A BOOK OF ONE'S OWN

LUCY McCARRAHER

R3THINK PRESS

First published in Great Britain 2019
by Rethink Press (www.rethinkpress.com)

Cover design by Clementine Keith-Roach

Illustrations by Lucy McCarraher

Printed and bound by CPI Group (UK) Ltd, Croydon, CR0 4YY

Contents

For all the women authors who have written their business books, and all those who will. You are all heroes and you make a difference.

'Women have sat indoors all these millions of years, so that by this time the very walls are permeated by their creative force, which has, indeed, so overcharged the capacity of bricks and mortar that it must needs harness itself to pens and brushes and business and politics.'

Virginia Woolf, *A Room of One's Own*

Foreword

Writing a book had been a dream for many years but, like a lot of women, I put it off. I didn't know how, and I couldn't justify investing in myself to find out. Now, don't get me wrong, I was happy to invest in many things: new technology, a new website, pretty much anything other than training for myself.

Then one day I read a post by Tim Ferriss (for those of you who follow him, his posts are loooong) and he was talking about a one-off event that he was going to run to teach people how to write a best-selling book. I thought, f**ck it, if I'm going to do it, I'm doing it now and I'm going to learn from the best. I invested $10,000 to attend Tim Ferriss' Open the Kimono (OTK) workshop in Napa, California. The event was limited to 120 places and you had to apply, be interviewed and accepted in order to get a place. At the time I didn't even have a fully-fledged book idea, so understandably most of my friends thought I was crazy.

But I knew this was what I needed to do in order to literally make me take action. It turned out to be the best investment I ever made. I wrote *Stop Talking, Start Doing* and the rest, as they say, is history. Three #1 best-selling books later, I'm a *Sunday Times* best-seller, and my next book is due to be published in 2019.

The truth is, I have never found it hard being a woman in business, but I also realise that I am one of the lucky ones. Whilst I have had many more than my fair share of challenges, I have always had a very deep-rooted, unshakeable confidence. I have also been fortunate to have been supported throughout my career by some incredible men and women. Not everyone has the same luck. Many women have to work twice as hard to get half as far, and that needs to change – on every level and in every sector, and until it does our work is not done.

Writing a book gave me the kind of credibility that is hard to put into words, and certainly the greatest door-opener I could ask for. When I work with women starting up their own businesses, I always encourage them to write their own book as I know it is one of the things that will make the biggest difference – and I often recommend they work with Lucy to do so. But many of them put it off, like I did, or are reluctant to take that time for themselves, or make their views public.

This has to stop.

By bringing together the stories of over fifty female authors, Lucy has shown us that we are not alone. Most of us go through the same anxiety, lack of confidence and reluctance to make that investment in time and money to write and publish our book. The stories of these fifty women show us how, when they took the plunge, it was life-changing for them, their businesses and their families; how their investment paid off in so many ways. Just like it did for me.

Lucy is the go-to mentor for business book writing and in this book, she takes you through writing and publishing a successful book step-by-step in exactly the same way she does with the hundreds of authors that she has worked with personally.

I've always been a champion for diversity and I was shocked to find that not a single woman author was picked as a winner in the first Business Book Awards. Unless we get more women out there writing books and putting them forward, this won't change. So I am going to do everything I can to encourage more of you to get that book out of your head… and into reality.

A Book of One's Own is valuable reading for men and women; everyone needs to be aware of the conscious and unconscious bias that affects women. Whilst I was lucky to have bucked the trend, that doesn't mean that it doesn't exist.

We need more non-fiction books written by female authors: books of authority, books with meaning, books that serve. Let's work together to make that happen.

Shaa Wasmund MBE
Entrepreneur and #1 best-selling author of
Stop Talking, Start Doing

Introduction

'Have you any notion how many books are written about women in the course of one year? Have you any notion how many are written by men?'
Virginia Woolf, *A Room of One's Own*

I started my working life in publishing, had my first book – a business book – published in 2002, and co-founded Rethink Press – a hybrid publishing company for entrepreneur authors – in 2011. I've been writing and/or publishing all my life, and never given much thought to the gender balance of authors.

In 2017, I founded the Business Book Awards, to celebrate the best of business writing and publishing. I picked a Judging Panel of ten female and ten male authors, publishers and business experts. Head Judge Alison Jones and I (both women, obviously) formulated the entry categories and rigorous judging criteria, all of which we thought were balanced and fair. Our judges did a sterling job assessing the 150 books entered in our inaugural Awards. They followed the process with insight and integrity.

Our category winners, the winner of an additional Judges' Choice Award, and the winner of the overall Business Book of the Year Award were all experts in their field and great writers; their books were top quality. The author of every single one of our eleven award-winning books, including three co-authored books, was a white man.

After the Awards, I tracked back: of the 150 entries, one-third were from women authors; slightly less than a third of female-authored books had made it to the category short lists, and none to the list of winners.

At Rethink Press, authors approach us to publish their business and self-development books; we don't commission or seek out authors, so there is no mediation of types of book or author we publish. I'd assumed we published roughly equal amounts of men and women authors – but when I analysed our list, it was about one-third female to two-thirds male.

Why were so many fewer women than men writing books about their knowledge, experience and expertise in their market, business or sector, I wondered. Maybe, I guessed, for the same reasons that fewer women than men start their own businesses: they have less confidence than men in their own abilities, are more risk averse, and have to factor in caring responsibilities; they are also taken less seriously by external organisations and individuals, and lack role models, mentors and networks.

If that was the case, then ironically, writing and publishing their own book could be of particular benefit to women entrepreneurs: it confers an external authority and consolidates an internal confidence; it creates valuable intellectual property for their business; and it acts as a selling point for the company, the brand and the author themselves. Entrepreneurs who are the authors of good books increase their client base, raise their fees, get industry speaking gigs and gain more attention from the media. Women in business can profit from all of these outcomes, perhaps even more than men.

In 1929 Virginia Woolf, who had started her own publishing company, the Hogarth Press, published two lectures she gave to Oxford women's colleges under the title *A Room of One's Own*. In this short book she explored the topic of Women and Fiction, analysed the historical lack of novels by (and about) women, and famously advocated that 'a woman must have money and a room of her own if she is to write fiction.'

Ninety years later, in a different time and context, there is still a case to be made for women to write their books and benefit from publishing their stories, their experience and expertise. In a world where respect for women is sadly lacking, and unconscious as well as conscious bias undermines us, the authority of being a published author can raise respect for individual women and add to the sum of esteem for women in general.

My focus here is not on the type of book written by women authors who have achieved fame in business; although they play a vital role in turning the spotlight on important issues – like Mary Portas' excellent *Work Like a Woman* and Sheryl Sandberg's *Lean In* – they will sell in volume as the celebrity autobiographies they partially are. The books I am advocating for are those written by women staking out their territory in their own business arena, appealing to their own niche market.

Everyone I spoke to about what had become a mission for me was enthusiastic and wanted to add their voice and experience to inspire women entrepreneurs, coaches and consultants to put finger to keyboard and publish their book. Through a survey and extended interviews with over fifty women authors of business books, who have themselves overcome challenges like lack of self-confidence, money and time to write their books, publish and then leverage them with aplomb, I brought together the ABOO Circle. I wanted to hear from a wide range of women who had written, or were writing, their books, and have them contribute their views, stories, tips and techniques to *A Book of One's Own – a manifesto for women to share their experience and make a difference*. Quotes that are attributed to the authors are taken from recorded interviews (they will be available in full on the *A Book of One's Own* podcast); unattributed shorter quotes are from the ABOO survey. There is a full list of the ABOO Circle and their book titles at the end of this book.

With all their varied experience and insightful advice, these authors have helped me analyse the reasons why women can be hesitant to write their books; the benefits for them, their businesses, their families and society in writing their books; and why they should do their best to overcome fears and barriers to do so.

I offer, along with the ABOO Circle's contributions, research into business, entrepreneurship, the publishing industry, and neuroscience, and aspects of my own experience in mentoring and publishing hundreds of entrepreneur authors that can most support women through the planning, writing and publishing process. I also introduce some archetypes that women need to be aware of in their writing process, like The Impostor, Big Sister, The Twin, The Angel, The Librarian and Miss Moneypenny.

I hope men, as well as women, will find some insights here – about why the writing and publishing experience can be different for women to that of men; about why it's important and healthy for individuals, business and society to encourage women to write their books; and how we can deploy our unique mindsets to make the process as stress-free, quick and supported as it can be.

Part One

Big Sister Is Watching You

'Literature is strewn with the wreckage of those who have minded beyond reason the opinion of others.'

Virginia Woolf, *A Room of One's Own*

1

Why Women Don't Write Their Business Books

It was 1971 and I was seventeen, sitting on a train from Oxford to London. I opened my new copy of a book that had been causing a stir in the press and media, Germaine Greer's *The Female Eunuch*, and started reading. In that hour of travel, my perception of the world shifted radically and forever.

> 'Woman power means the self-determination of women, and that means that all the baggage of paternalist society will have to be thrown overboard. Woman… may never herself see the ultimate goal, for the fabric of society is not unravelled in a single lifetime, but she may state it as her belief and find hope in it.'
>
> **Germaine Greer, *The Female Eunuch***

Maybe it's hard for people younger than me to recapture what the world was like for women at that time. We couldn't take out a mortgage or a loan without male sponsorship; contraception was not available on the NHS and we were frequently made

9

redundant when we got pregnant; marital rape, domestic abuse and lower pay for women than men were legal; we were banned from working in the Stock Exchange and drinking in many pubs.[1]

On the one hand, it's gratifying to know that since then so much has been achieved towards an acceptance that women are the equal if not the facsimile of men, and that young women coming of age now take this for granted. On the other, in this era of #metoo and #timesup, we're seeing in graphic detail just how much has not changed, how 'the fabric of society is not unravelled in a single lifetime', and how much work there is still to do.

Stepping away from sexual abuse and harassment, it is well enough known that getting on in business is full of challenges for women. Sheryl Sandberg has documented the issues of being female in the corporate world and summarises one of the most corrosive:

> 'The gender stereotypes introduced in childhood are reinforced throughout our lives and become self-fulfilling prophesies. Most leadership positions are held by men, so women don't expect to achieve them, and that becomes one of the reasons they don't.'
>
> **Sheryl Sandberg, _Lean In: Women, Work, and the Will to Lead_**

---

1   http://www.bbc.co.uk/guides/zxb9g82#z9gkrdm

But even when we start and run our own businesses, there are still problems to contend with. I asked the fifty women authors of the ABOO Circle, who are all entrepreneurs, business founders and owners, coaches and consultants, whether being a woman had made their work or business journey harder.

- Sixteen women (33%) said it had made *no difference at all*

- Fifteen (31%) felt being a woman had affected them *a little*

- Eleven of the ABOO Circle (22%) had found their business journey harder by *a moderate amount*

- Four women (8%) said being a woman had made business *a lot* harder

- Three authors (6%) felt it had affected them *a great deal*

So, 67% of women authors who completed the ABOO survey said that their work or business journey had been made harder to some degree by their gender.

It is possible to put figures on the lower value 'the market' puts on women entrepreneurs. In March 2018, *The Telegraph* published an open letter[2] to the government signed by 200 women entrepreneurs, business leaders, MPs and academics to request better access for female founders of businesses in order to boost the UK economy. It described how female entrepreneurs are being held back by a lack of access to capital.

---

2 https://www.telegraph.co.uk/women/business/200-business-leaders-mps-sign-telegraph-letter-urging-government/

These are extraordinary figures:

- 9% of annual funding into UK start-ups currently goes to women-run businesses

- Women-led businesses are 86% less likely to be venture-capital funded than men-led businesses[3]

- Women-owned businesses win less than 5% of corporate and public sector contracts[4]

- Women are 56% less likely to secure angel investment

The All Party Parliamentary Group on Entrepreneurship's report on Women in Leadership[5] showed that women face barriers in accessing business funding via traditional routes as a result of unconscious bias. And research from Harvard Business School[6] revealed that a woman pitching for funds dramatically reduces the odds of a company receiving investment: male entrepreneurs were rated as being more persuasive, fact-based and logical – even when the pitches from both genders were identical.

---

3 https://www.home.barclays/content/dam/barclayspublic/docs/ BarclaysNews/2017/Mar/0001_FFF_AccesstoFinanceScaleUp_AWK_ WEB.pdf

4 NPCWE / Prowess 'Procurement: Fostering Equal Access for Women's Enterprise, 2009'

5 https://static1.squarespace.com/static/58ed40453a04116f46e8d99b/t/5b5 2e7d203ce640bec5e6800/1532159970548/006_APPG_Women_Online. pdf

6 http://gap.hks.harvard.edu/investors-prefer-entrepreneurial-ventures-pitched-attractive-men

Female participation in business ownership is directly associated with higher credit rejection probability. In 2016, 86% of deals involved companies without a single female founder, while 14% involved companies with at least one woman in charge. In the same year, 91% of investment by value was directed into companies without a single female founder, while just 9% went to companies with at least one.

In her TEDx Talk 'The real reason female entrepreneurs get less funding'[7], Dana Kanze, a doctoral fellow at Columbia Business School who applies behavioural insights to understand sources of inequality in entrepreneurship, describes why she believes that although 38% of US companies are founded by women, they receive only 2% of the venture funding. 'Regulatory Focus', a social psychological theory by Professor Tory Higgins[8], differentiates between two distinct motivational orientations of promotion and prevention. Promotion focus is concerned with positive gains, goals, hopes and accomplishment, while a prevention focus is concerned with losses, safety, responsibility and security needs. In interviews by both men and women venture capitalists, 67% of questions to male entrepreneurs were promotion-focused, while 66% of those asked of female entrepreneurs were prevention-focused. These allowed the men seeking funding to respond in positive terms about the future of their business, while women entrepreneurs were forced to defend themselves against

---

7   https://www.ted.com/talks/dana_kanze_the_real_reason_female_
    entrepreneurs_get_less_funding#t-651037

8   https://www0.gsb.columbia.edu/mygsb/faculty/research/pubfiles/529/
    HIGGINSADVANCES_1998REG_FOC_.pdf

negative questioning. This gender-biased questioning strongly affected the funding outcomes.

And this is despite the fact that those women who have been able to beat the odds and secure finance for their business are performing better than male-dominated companies:

- Women entrepreneurs bring in 20% more revenue with 50% less money invested

- Only 23% of businesses founded by women entrepreneurs fail, compared with 34% of those founded by men

- Since 2011, investments into companies with no female directors on their board average £2.9m, whereas adding a single female board member corresponds with a typical increase of £500,000[9]

- When business characteristics (size, sector, age, funding) are controlled for, women-owned firms outperform those owned by their male counterparts[10]

When are people – men and other women – going to notice that we're smart at business, sharp with money, and have snappy ideas?

And that's part of the problem. Women expect people to notice our good work and hopefully reward us for it; we don't like to, and don't think we should need to, point out our achievements

9 https://www.forbes.com/sites/davidprosser/2017/03/27/eight-stats-that-show-how-britain-fails-its-female-entrepreneurs/#3a82208574bd
10 Women in Enterprise: A Different Perspective. RBS Group 2012

or ask for recompense and recognition. But this is not the way the world – the male-dominated world – works.

'As research reveals, men are four times more likely to ask for higher pay than are women with the same qualifications. From career promotions to help with child care, studies show time and again that women don't ask – and frequently don't even realize that they can.'

> **Linda Babcock and Sara Laschever, *Women Don't Ask: The High Cost of Avoiding Negotiation – And Positive Strategies for Change***

Donna Whitbrook, co-author of *Trusted – The human approach to building outstanding client relationships in a digitised world*, remembers back to her corporate days:

'If I reflect back to when I was a senior manager with Nationwide Building Society, I can recall having a moment once, thinking, "Who are all these men jumping over my head here? What is going on?" Because I knew that I was top of my game in terms of performance and the results that I brought, and in terms of my work ethic. What I realised was that men were leapfrogging because I wasn't saying, "I'm ready for this promotion now. I'm ready to step into this." It wasn't around my lack of confidence; it was probably around me thinking that I was going to sit and wait for someone to hand me that lovely tiara, put it on my head and say, "There you are. We've brought you a nice promotion".'

The ABOO Circle says:

'We have less confidence in our knowledge and expertise.'

'We are trained to be helpful, not pushy.'

'Although I've been in sales my whole life, it's not only women, but it shows up more extensively in women, this feeling that if you were to sell something, you would have to turn into something quite horrible in order to be successful. And there's a perception, I've found, over the last few decades, that the reason particularly women don't like selling is they believe that they would have to become that person, you know, that creepy, slimy, foot-in-the-doorway kind of salesperson. And, for many of them, it turns them off.'

Audrey Chapman, author, *Love Selling: how to sell without selling out*

Can publishing a book help a woman to be noticed in an incompatible business culture where normative behaviour for 'winners' is to display supreme confidence in their not necessarily supreme abilities, and to actively sell themselves rather than being noticed for their success?

I spoke to Daniel Priestley, bestselling author of four books and founder of Dent Global, which runs the Threshold Accelerator for entrepreneurs whose business turnover is below the VAT threshold (£83,000 in 2018), and the Key Person of Influence programme for entrepreneurs with generally a six-figure and above turnover. We started from the assumption that women and men are equally talented writers, that most business book authors are significantly experienced in their own area, and that they have a business that would benefit from them writing an authoritative book. With that as the basis, he questioned whether business book authorship was simply divided by gender in proportion to the number of businesses run by men and women. For example, if only 15% of such businesses are run by women and 15% of this type of author are women, then the problem becomes less how to get more women to write their book, and more how to get more wore women founding and running businesses.

'If there's a disparity in proportional representation, then I'd be speculating on what might be causing it. Research I'm aware of suggests differences between male and female entrepreneurs that could be relevant:

Women are three times more likely to be running a business part time (17% of men vs 53% women[11]): this skews the numbers of female entrepreneurs and explains why women are more likely to have smaller businesses than men. It may also explain why women don't want to commit to another time-intensive task. Women are less likely than men to accept risk.

---

11   ONS Labour Market Statistics, September 2014

All things being equal, women are more likely to be offered debt funding from a bank. However, they are less likely to take on the loan than a man offered the exact same terms.[12] A book might be seen as a risky move financially because it has a cost of time and money attached without any clear indication as to the payoff – you could release it and it could flop; even worse, it could attract criticism. Women are more likely to start a business out of "necessity" and men are more likely to start a business based on "opportunity". This might suggest that some women are reluctant entrepreneurs and aren't necessarily trying to go all-in on their industry.

Linked to this is that women's goals from business are more likely to be "lifestyle/flexibility" whereas men are more likely to say they want "growth/performance/to be number one". This slight difference could also have implications for book writing.'

I asked the ABOO Circle, 'Why do you think fewer women than men write and publish business books?'

- Six women authors (13%) felt that women view it as *taking a bigger risk*

- Nine respondents (19%) said it felt like *a selfish use of our time*

---

12   Carter, S & Shaw, E, 'Women's Business Ownership', report to SBS/ DTI 2006

- Ten women (21%) said it was because *there are fewer women in business*

- Twenty-six ABOO authors (54%) felt it was because *we have less confidence in our knowledge and expertise*

- Twenty-seven women (56%) said *finding the time to write* was an issue

- Twenty-nine respondents (60%) said it was because *we find it hard to put ourselves out there*

The following words and phrases featured most in their comments:

The ABOO Circle said:

> 'Culturally, women self-promoting is seen as showing off, whereas culturally it's admirable confidence in a man.'

> 'It's more of the same reasons women are behind men in many areas. We think we can't, so we don't. Men think they can, and they do!'

'Not enough role models being encouraging.'

'I think when women have children, that quite rightly takes up the majority of time. If you are running a business as well, finding time to write on top of that might be very difficult. I didn't have children and see my books as my babies. Many of my friends would love to write books but are just too busy.'

2

Feel The Fear And Do It Anyway

'A self-assured woman who is in control of her life draws like a magnet. She is so filled with positive energy that people want to be around her.'

Susan Jeffers, *Feel The Fear And Do It Anyway*

In 1987, an unknown American psychologist called Susan Jeffers published a radical self-help book called *Feel The Fear And Do It Anyway* – *how to turn your fear and indecision into confidence and action.* Her simple but profound advice changed the lives of millions of people; it helped them overcome their fears and heal the pain in their lives.

She asked:

'What is it for you? Fear of… public speaking, asserting yourself, making decisions, intimacy, changing jobs, being alone, aging, driving, losing a loved one, ending a relationship? Is it some of the above? All of the above? Perhaps you could add a few more to the list.'[13]

---

13 Susan Jeffers, *Feel The Fear And Do It Anyway: How to Turn Your Fear and Indecision into Confidence and Action* 25th edition, Ebury Publishing 2012

Susan Jeffers didn't include 'writing and publishing a book' in her list, and although she might have felt the fear of that, she did it anyway. It is good advice, and she is a great role model and advisor.

When women are feeling the fear of taking a big step, committing to a substantial project or doing something that will put us in the public view, we tend to fall into typical thought patterns that we use to justify not being brave. Here are three archetypes we should be wary of when they start trying to dissuade us from setting out on our writing journey.

The Risk Assessor

The Risk Assessor has total prevention focus and is on constant alert for potential downsides to any action. The Book sets off alarms for her on many levels.

'Having to expose yourself to potential failure can be super tough – I believe that women, more than men, consider this aspect far more deeply.'

Jane Frankland, author of *IN Security – Why a Failure to Attract and Retain Women in Cybersecurity is Making Us All Less Safe*, has done extensive research on perceptions of risk in women and men for her area of expertise. In her book, she says:

'Countless studies have shown that women and men gauge risk differently. Women are far better at assessing odds than men, and this often manifests itself as an increased avoidance of risk. As women are typically more risk averse, their natural detailed exploration makes them more attuned to changing pattern behaviours – a skill that's needed for correctly identifying threat actors and protecting environments.'[14]

The message of Jane's book was a challenge to her industry – because women are fundamentally different to men, when it comes to cybersecurity, if a company or the industry as a whole is short on women, it's less safe. *IN Security* puts the case for women in cybersecurity because of the way they view and deal with risk. Typically, women are more risk averse, compliant with rules, and embracing of organisational controls and technology than men. They're also extremely intuitive and score highly when it comes to

14 Jane Frankland, *IN Security – Why a Failure to Attract and Retain Women in Cybersecurity is Making Us All Less Safe*. Rethink Press, 2017.

emotional and social intelligence, which enables them to remain calm during times of turbulence – a trait that's required when major security breaches and incidents occur. With cybercrime, terrorism and warfare increasing, Jane saw the number of women in cybersecurity actually declining, so her book was a wake-up call to action.

With full awareness of our gender's predisposition to evaluate risk more highly, and having the assurance of her market and publishers that her book was wanted, needed and important, Jane herself still felt that the risk in writing and publishing her views might be too great.

> 'I went through a whole process of actually being quite insecure, and the irony is my book is called *IN Security*. I went through that process of "is it good enough? Is it ready?" I'm sure I'm not alone among first-time authors going through that process, and, particularly, I think, women because we have more of a tendency to want everything to be perfect, and then, of course, we're judged more, especially if we are in a minority.
>
> I'm in cyber security, so it's a minority space. My market was dying for the book; they couldn't wait for it. And, that just made me more worried about whether it was going to be good enough. I wanted to be sure it would help, and so I went through that whole process of procrastination and holding back.'

Jane took over a year to write her book, and mitigated her feelings of risk by doing extensive research to support her claims. In the end she included some 200 data reference points, so her theories couldn't be challenged. Because she also wanted her book to be really accessible, she told lots of stories, beginning each chapter with an anecdote of her own, and then illustrating her points with stories from other people, some women, some men.

'They were from the whole ecosystem as well, so I didn't just want people who were at the top, particularly women at the top of their game. I wanted to really pull in voices throughout the ecosystem and from all over the world, so that's how I tackled it. And what people have said to me is that they really enjoyed it, because it wasn't just a book full of stories. Every single thing that I wrote about was backed up with hard data.'

However, Jane's assessment of the risk involved in challenging her industry was not wrong. Although her book has been very positively received, had excellent reviews, and she's received thanks from many women who now don't feel so alone in the cybersecurity industry, there was some backlash. Jane attended an industry event in 2018 and called out the presence of 'booth babes' – scantily dressed young women 'selling' products on company stands – a throwback tactic that hadn't been seen for some time and was contrary to the rules of the event. Jane tweeted, calling out the event organiser and the company in question, so that they could take action, and everyone received an apology.

A journalist picked up the story and wrote about it, and then it took off on Twitter. Because Jane had a high profile in the industry, through her book and other work, she was viciously trolled for days. Eventually, some people were banned from Twitter and others were reprimanded by their employers for saying what they did, and a resolution was reached.

> 'So a lot of good came out of it, but I did notice that women are targeted more for speaking out. They're targeted by men and women, so it's a hard environment and you need a support mechanism around you to actually help you with that. Many people reached out to me and said, "Are you OK?" or "I'm too frightened to comment" or "I'm worried about putting fuel on the fire" or "I might get into trouble from my employer if I comment". Luckily, I knew I had supporters in the background, so I just bore the brunt of it, then dealt with the trolls and those who were bringing their own agenda to social media.'

Since then, Jane has set up a new initiative: a code of conduct for future events, which has been backed by major event organisers and leaders in her industry. Aligning with the Time's Up movement and NOW Australia, the code of conduct's purpose is to ensure that all people, particularly women, are kept safe from inappropriate behaviour, such as bullying, harassment and assault at events.

Big Sister

Big Sister feels indispensable and responsible for
everyone's wellbeing, professional and personal,
in her business and at home.

'An extraordinary sense of responsibility, a tendency to
take the lead, a fear of making mistakes, being hit hard by
criticism, and caring for others to the point of exhaustion…'

Lisette Schuitemaker and Wies Enthoven,
The Eldest Daughter Effect

I first met Lisette Schuitemaker when we were both eight years
old, and her family came to stay with mine at our holiday house
in Aldeburgh. Our mothers had both been at the University of
Geneva soon after the war, after which they both worked briefly,
then married and started families. Their first children, both girls,
were born exactly a month apart, followed by two more children
each, of similar ages (and the Schuitemakers later had another boy).

I don't know whose idea it was to get an English and a Dutch family, who had never met and didn't even share a common language, to spend two weeks together in close conditions, but luckily I and the other eldest daughter, Lisette, took to each other immediately. We tried to keep our much less well-matched siblings in order, used car journeys to teach them songs in both languages, and created an English-Dutch dictionary for our own use.

Lisette and I both became writers. Her third book is an extraordinary piece of work called *The Eldest Daughter Effect*. In it, she analyses a research project she and her co-author Wies Enthoven undertook with a group of first-born women, and describes how eldest daughters have a recognisable combination of characteristics that defines their behaviour, draws them to each other, and also makes them vulnerable to other people's demands and reactions.

Lisette summarises eldest daughters:

> 'Of course, first and foremost, it's like our middle name is Responsible: before anything else, we are the responsible ones. We are charged with responsibility and we're used to taking responsibility, which also makes us sometimes a bit bossier than we think we are. But we think we're responsible for everything and everyone. And the second characteristic is that we are incredibly dutiful. If we say we will do something, we will do it, come what may. If we are responsible for looking after someone, or some people, we must and will do it to the best of our ability. Then we are

"hands-on" – we feel bound to take action. And we are thoughtful and, finally, caring.'

Eldest daughters tend to be perfectionists, are generally very susceptible to criticism and judgement, and equally other people's praise and approbation matters to them enormously. Yet even if they are told they've done well, first-born women are likely to see faults in everything they've done. They worry about all the work they have to do in the future, yet belittle their own achievements in the past.

When I read Lisette and Wies' book for the first time, it was like taking a personality test that explained rationally why you are who you are: revealing, reassuring and relieving. And yet, this description of an eldest daughter could apply to almost any woman – regardless of where she sits in her family of origin – who has started or is running her own business. Every woman entrepreneur I know, on founding their business defaults to a role that is very like a big sister: she feels personally responsible for the wellbeing of her clients or customers, the security of her employees or colleagues, and the satisfaction of her associates and partners, to the degree that they become her family, or one of her families.

Interestingly, Lisette tells me that in her experience of talking at conferences of international women's networks, about half the entrepreneur delegates are usually eldest daughters.

'We resemble one another in the deep-rooted belief that we could safeguard our place by being good and performing well. We are alike in our conclusion that, as the eldest, we needed to uphold the rules of the house and had to take care of the rest. We are similar in our conviction that we are responsible. That if we don't do it... ' [15]

And if the businesswoman also has a family:

'She wants to be a good mother as well as have a high-flying job, be the perfect partner for the love of her life as well as a trusted friend whose door is always open.'

So, to take time out from her responsibilities to her 'younger siblings' in order to write extensively about her own ideas, practices and views can feel uncomfortable and inappropriate to the 'Big Sister'. With nearly one-fifth of the ABOO Circle reporting that they thought women considered writing their book to be a 'selfish use of their time', I have to wonder whether this is a factor that would inhibit a man.

'I didn't feel that at all, but I do have a lot of clients I discuss this exact topic with in regard to looking after yourself and wellbeing. Because a lot of people feel really guilty about taking time out for themselves, to go for a massage or a yoga class or something. And I suppose I've

---

15   Lisette Schuitemaker, *The Eldest Daughter Effect: how first-born women – like Oprah Winfrey, Sheryl Sandberg, JK Rowling and Beyoncé – harness their strengths*. Inner Traditions/Bear & Company, 2016.

selfishly always made time for that. And similarly, I wanted to write the book, so I've made time for it.'

Donna Whitbrook, co-author, *Trusted*

The Twin – if I were a boy...

We all have a phantom male twin – we get disheartened because we know he would get noticed and taken more seriously than we are.

'Women have served all these centuries as looking glasses possessing the magic and delicious power of reflecting the figure of man at twice its natural size.'

Virginia Woolf, *A Room of One's Own*

Ten of the ABOO Circle thought that the number of women business authors compared to the number of men was simply a function of the relative numbers of business owners of each gender. There are more male entrepreneurs than female, so the numbers of business books written and published are relative to that imbalance. There are twice as many male entrepreneurs as female in the UK, and in my experience, there is the same proportion of men business authors to women.

But is that an over-simplification? One ABOO Circle contributor suggested:

> 'There are fewer women on the courses and events that suggest that writing a book is achievable. I thought the only route was via Penguin or Wiley and did not know how to move forward. Actually, with small publishers and self-publishing there are no barriers. This is where a good publisher can guide the process.'

Marianne Page, author of *Process to Profit* and *Simple, Logical, Repeatable*, suggests that even on such programmes, women and men take different attitudes to the challenge of writing their book.

> 'The whole process of writing the book was interesting, because I was watching people around me on the accelerator programme, particularly the men. They were sort of churning out these books really quickly, and I was spending a long time getting everything down in as much detail as I could, and going back and writing and rewriting. And I do think that, in a sort of men versus

women thing, one of the difficulties is that we tend to be more the perfectionists. We want to make sure that it's right. We want to be absolutely confident that these words of ours that are going out into the wider domain are going to be worth reading.

In the group I was in, there were a few men who – I was going to be disrespectful and say they dashed out a book, but that is how it felt to me at the time. They wrote their book fast, got their name on it, and then were very confident in the promotion of it. They were going to be *New York Times* Best Sellers – that was the way they promoted their own book, and to great effect as well. They got fantastic reviews, they got lots of people helping them to promote, and I think, on reflection, that would be the difference between them and me as a woman.'

Many ABOO authors agreed that women tend to have less confidence in their expertise and knowledge, and a higher degree of perfectionism (or simply wanting to get it right) when they expose their views to the wider world. However, the wider world also seems to regard women's books as literally of less value than those of men.

A couple of ABOO respondents reported some experience of that:

'Publishers may have an unconscious bias towards proposals by men.'

'Resistance from agents and publishers, especially if writing on "male" topics like economics and leadership.'

In an extensive piece of research published in April 2018, spanning the years 2002 to 2012 and including over two million book titles, Dana B Weinberg and Adam Kapelner compared discrimination mechanisms and inequality in indie and traditional publishing. They found that in the traditional publishing industry over all, books by female authors are priced 45% lower than those of male authors and women-authored books are under-represented in the more prestigious genres. The pricing disparity falls to 7% in indie and self-publishing, but is still apparent.

'… the book industry illuminates how the gig economy may disrupt, replicate, or transform the gender discrimination mechanisms and inequality found in the traditional economy. We find that indie publishing, though more egalitarian, largely replicates traditional publishing's gender discrimination patterns, showing an unequal distribution of male and female authors by genre (allocative discrimination), devaluation of genres written predominantly by female authors (valuative discrimination), and lower prices within genres for books by female authors (within-job discrimination).'[16]

16 Weinberg DB, Kapelner A (2018) 'Comparing gender discrimination and inequality in indie and traditional publishing'. PLoS ONE 13(4): e0195298. https://doi.org/10.1371/journal.pone.0195298

The authors of the report also point out that there are more women writing in genres such as romance, which are generally priced lower than male-dominated genres such as science (why?). But even after accounting for these differences, they found that prices for authors with identifiably female names were 9% lower than for male authors. The annual VIDA counts of book reviews show there is still a much higher number of reviews of books by male authors, written by male reviewers.[17]

It seems like a long time since Charlotte, Emily and Anne Brontë felt the need to write under the male pseudonyms Currer, Ellis, and Acton Bell; since Mary Anne Evans had to call herself George Eliot; or even since Nelle Harper Lee dropped her first name to achieve literary fame. But it is not that long ago that Joanne Rowling's publisher asked her to use the author name JK Rowling, in case young boys were put off an adventure story of a young male magician by its author being a woman, and that she took the pen name Robert Galbraith for her adult crime novels. And UK publishers of Jodi Picoult's book *Small Great Things* sent out proofs without her name or a title attached, and with the tagline #readwithoutprejudice. It was a clever bit of marketing, but it also played into assumptions that women are the authors of 'commercial' fiction, as opposed to men who write serious literary fiction.

---

17 http://www.vidaweb.org/the-2017-vida-count/

Author Catherine Nichols was getting no response from agents she submitted her novel to, so, although 'the plan made me feel dishonest and creepy', she re-sent out her manuscript under a male name.

> 'I sent the six queries I had planned to send that day. Within 24 hours, George had five responses – three manuscript requests and two warm rejections praising his exciting project. For contrast, under my own name, the same letter and pages sent 50 times had netted me a total of two manuscript requests... Total data: George sent out 50 queries, and had his manuscript requested 17 times. He is eight and a half times better than me at writing the same book. Fully a third of the agents who saw his query wanted to see more, where my numbers never did shift from one in 25.'[18]

I asked my co-founder and business partner, Joe Gregory, whether, in his publishing career before or since we started Rethink Press, he had noticed a difference in male and female authors or their books. We had never discussed this before, so I was quite surprised that he had an instant answer to this question:

> 'This is a generalisation, and I'm going from my own thinking, how I see things and the way I operate. I think men are better bullshitters. We can kind of bluff our way a little bit, and feel comfortable bluffing, when actually we don't really know what we're talking about. The women

---

18   https://jezebel.com/homme-de-plume-what-i-learned-sending-my-novel-out-und-1720637627

I've worked with and the women I know tend to be a bit more cautious about blowing their own trumpet or saying something with certainty, unless they are certain. I think what happens then is more men think "I should write a book on this, because what I've got to say is bloody brilliant," maybe with not quite as much substance as a female author might bring.

Again, I'm generalising, and I'm not picking on any of our authors in particular, but I'd say the case is we publish a lot of books that are the individual's ideas, and they don't necessarily need the back-up of facts and figures and research. When we tend to work with female authors, a lot of their books seem to be much better supported with actual facts rather than just opinion, so those are harder books to write, it takes longer, and there's more fear of getting it wrong. Manuscripts by women tend to be more well thought out and more conscientious in terms of "What we're handing over is our best work" rather than "This is what I've got, now you can make it better".'

Another generalisation we have noticed at Rethink Press is that when we return heavily edited manuscripts to their male authors, their response is often a bit surprised and initially miffed, while female authors tend to instruct us to be very rigorous with the editing and are grateful for our intensive intervention when we improve their work. It strikes me that this follows a (very general) pattern that men can be more confident in their views and their writing abilities, even when this may not be entirely justified, and less worried about the response or judgement; while women are less secure in their book's content and their writing style, and more anxious about the criticism they might receive.

Antoinette Oglethorpe, whose book *Grow Your Geeks* is a model of strong, original content and clear writing, is an example of the latter:

'I think it stems from childhood. I remember at the end of one summer, we'd had to write what we did in our holidays. And we hadn't done very much actually, so I wrote a very factual half-page of A4 about what I'd done in my holidays. It was a creative writing exercise and I wasn't very creative. And I remember my mum and the headmistress having a bit of a giggle about this.

And then when I did my O-levels, again I got good grades in English, but my worst grade of my O-levels was English language. My sister thought it was hilarious that my lowest grade was in my own language. And I always felt my father judged me based on my grades and my salary. I suppose these are all little things – but the fact that I remember them forty-five years on shows that they have an impact on my confidence and my belief in my writing ability. Which is probably at odds with my actually ability.

I went to an all-girls school, I had a sister, so I never really had the comparatives of gender. But I don't think this is unique to my upbringing. As I've grown older and

I've moved into the world of the training environment, which is associated with HR and predominantly female dominated, I see a reluctance to speak up and speak out. I talk to other very well qualified and experienced women, clients as well as colleagues, and they say things like, "Oh, I could never write a book, I don't have anything to say".'

Back to the Big Sister scenario. Joe is the youngest and only brother of three elder sisters, so has 'seen a lot of women interaction' over the years. As an entrepreneur, he has always worked with women on an equal footing, so perhaps has a reasonably objective view of how women and men function. Here's his honest, male, and not particularly complimentary to either side, take on how the different genders operate:

'If you act like a knob and you're a woman, other women will know you're a knob and call you out on it. If you do it as a man, it's like we all know everybody else is doing it, so nobody really gives it a second thought. I've got no research or data to back this up, but I would imagine it is scarier for women, because women interact differently to men. I think women hold each other to higher account than men tend to, so there's less opportunity to just bluff it and say, "Well, you know, nobody will call me on it." Men have the privilege of, "Oh, it's a man, he must know what he's on about," and women have always had to kind of justify and prove themselves, even when they're completely equal, so their attitude is, "I can't mess this up, I don't want to get this wrong."

This may have happened unconsciously with the Business Book Awards: if there are two books, absolutely equal, nothing to choose between them, even when the judging panel is equally men and women, I just think the man's going to get the advantage, for no fair reason. Which means that if a woman writes a book, it's got to be bloody brilliant; it's got to be better than an average man's book. I think that, sadly, is true. I don't think it's an imagined reality.'

It's not just the Business Book Awards. Unfortunately, we're in good (or high-profile) company. Women authors win fewer book awards across the genres, and for no better reason, it seems, than that they are taken less seriously than men authors.

Margaret Atwood was the bestselling literary novelist of the year in *The Bookseller*'s 2017 Top Ten[19], followed by Sarah Perry, Helen Dunmore, Naomi Alderman, and Elena Feranti. Haruki Murakami, at number six, was the only male author, with the list completed by Ali Smith, Zadie Smith, Maggie O'Farrell and Arundhati Roy. It is estimated that more than two-thirds of fiction in the UK is bought by women, 60% of fiction is written by women, and novels that address our current preoccupations have done fantastically well recently: Margaret Atwood's

---

19 https://www.thebookseller.com/insight/atwood-leads-woman-dominated-literary-top-10-707621

The Handmaid's Tale[20] topped the best-seller lists, and Naomi Alderman's *The Power* (highly recommended) won the 2017 Baileys Prize and came first on Barack Obama's Books of the Year list. But the author Kamila Shamsie revealed that less than 40% of titles submitted by publishers for the Booker Prize in the previous five years had been by women, and of those, most had already been recognised by the Women's Prize for Fiction (launched in 1996 by women, for women to counteract the male bias in other literary prizes, and initially sponsored by Orange).[21]

She said:

> 'The list also underscores the bias at play when prize submissions, book recommendations by other writers, and reviews of literary fiction are so skewed towards men. That skewing isn't about quality, or about the opinions of the reading public – it's about gender bias that treats male writers as more "serious", even if women writers are more popular among the (largely female) readership for fiction.'

It is also notable that novels in which the main character is female win far fewer prizes than those with a man as the protagonist.

---

20 My editor, Alison Jack, left me the following note in regard to this title: 'Lucy – interestingly, when I googled this book, the first result that popped up told me it was an American TV series created by a man, only afterwards adding that the programme was based on the novel by Margaret Atwood.'

21 https://www.theguardian.com/books/2015/jun/05/ kamila-shamsie-2018-year-publishing-women-no-new-books-men

Aamna Mohdin of Quartz[22] listed the percentage of female winners of the top international book prizes up to 2016, which includes the following depressing statistics:

- Prix Goncourt – 11%

- Nobel Prize – 12%

- National Book Award (fiction) – 25%

- Pulitzer Prize (fiction) – 34%

- Man Booker Prize – 35%

In 1998, the appropriately named Francine Prose wrote an essay called 'Scent of a Woman's Ink'[23] in which she pointed out that there is an inherent bias in the way men's and women's fiction are perceived: for instance, when a male author writes about a family, it's regarded as social commentary, but when a female author addresses this subject, it's a story of domestic life. Twenty years later, not enough has changed in the authority that women's writing is accorded by women, men, reviewers and the judges of literary competitions, whether it's fiction or non-fiction.

---

22 https://www.theatlas.com/charts/r1gxer0lx
23 https://harpers.org/archive/1998/06/scent-of-a-womans-ink

3

What Held You Back?

I asked the ABOO Circle, 'When you first considered writing your book, what, if anything, held *you* back?'

- Five women authors (11%) said *caring or domestic responsibilities*

- Nine respondents (19%) felt that *lack of role models, mentors or supportive networks* had held them back

- Eighteen women (38%) cited *lack of confidence*

- Eighteen (38%) said *fear of failure*

- And a further eighteen (38%) had been held back by *not being taken seriously*

Words and phrases that came up regularly in their comments include:

The more detailed comments fell into three main areas, the first of which was around the fear women feel of judgement, criticism and ridicule.

The Impostor

The Impostor tries to play the game and play it cool, but
is always anxious that she'll be called out as a fraud.

'Did I have enough to say of importance? Was it unique
enough?'

'What was holding me back was a sense that it needed to
be perfect, and the fear of judgement.'

'Being criticised.'

'Impostor syndrome, the overwhelming number of diet
books already available, thinking I had nothing to say.'

Dr Tara Halliday is an expert in Impostor Syndrome, so much so that she wrote the book on it (notice how that phrase automatically connects authorship and expertise). *Unmasking: The Coach's Guide to Impostor Syndrome* was written for business coaches to help them identify an issue that 70% of their clients are likely to suffer from to varying degrees.[24] Then there is another 30% of highly successful people who don't recognise that they have Impostor Syndrome – which between the two adds up to pretty much all high achievers.

Tara discovered through her own research that she was in the 30%.

'I could see in myself some of the common traits: the tendency for perfectionism, the reviewing of events and discussions, and some element of a fear of failure, but I didn't see it as Impostor Syndrome until I was actually interviewed by somebody and they asked that question.

"So have you experienced Impostor Syndrome?"

And I replied, "No, actually I haven't." But then afterwards, I thought, "You know, I really have".

A lot of the 30% people don't recognise it because most successful people are generally confident and capable, as I was. But, when I looked at the idea of leadership – ah, that's where it showed up. So sometimes it only shows up in one

---

24 G. M. Matthews, 'Impostor Phenomenon: Attributions for Success and Failure', paper presented at American Psychological Association, Toronto, 1984.

particular area. For me, it was leadership, and then it was clear as day.'

This caused Tara to review her whole career, and she saw that her Impostor Syndrome had caused her to shy away from all offers of serious leadership, from self-sabotaging herself ('getting rip-roaring drunk') before an election for a Students' Union position to turning down offers of jobs leading teams and walking away from a super fast-track management position. She says it was a way of 'keeping myself small'; of not stepping up to fulfil a big leadership role.

> 'When you start looking at it, the stories come again and again. You think, "Oh my gosh. There it is and there it is and there it is." And it really was. In writing the book, I found out an awful lot about myself, which was wonderful.'

I expected Tara to tell me that there was a gender bias within Impostor Syndrome and that more women suffer from it than men, but she firmly denied that this is the case. Although initial research into the subject appeared to show that it did affect more women than men, the study turned out not to have been conducted on an anonymous basis. When later studies were anonymised, the results showed that men and women came out as equally susceptible. The only difference was that men wouldn't admit publicly to feeling Impostor Syndrome, while women would put their hands up to it.

So, if women are claiming that a sense of Impostor Syndrome holds them back from writing their books, is this in fact simply them being more open about something that men are just as likely to feel? And how does this square with the sort of received wisdom about men and women that Tom Schuller reflects in his powerful book, *The Paula Principle*?

> 'The consensus, from my interviewees and from recruitment specialists, was so clear that it leads me to offer the 60/20 confidence–competence axiom: men will consider themselves qualified for a job if they reckon they can do at least 60% of it; women will disqualify themselves if they believe there is 20% of the job that they can't do.'[25]

Tara believes that, both in terms of women writing books and women putting themselves forward in general, this comes back to a cultural bias of the framework that we operate within. For example, the same behaviour is interpreted differently when exhibited by the different genders: what in a man is taken as strong confidence is seen as arrogance in a woman because it is judged against an implicit expectation – an unconscious bias – of how women should be. Our culture still holds that women should not promote themselves because their role is as the consensus builders, the family builders, the community builders. We falsely believe that a woman should not be the one who stands alone and leads everyone else from the front – that is a job for men.

---

25 Schuller, Tom. *The Paula Principle: how and why women work below their level of competence.* Scribe Publications, 2017

'Where I totally fell down was insane Impostor Syndrome just as I went to publish. I almost didn't do it. I had to work through it with not one, but two coaches! And still, a part of me loathes being exposed in the way that writing a book exposes you. I just didn't see that coming. Because of these feelings of inadequacy, I still haven't done much at all in the way of marketing.'

So, when women do put themselves into a leadership role – which is what the author of a book is doing, stepping into a position of authority – that is where they experience Impostor Syndrome. It's not about their knowledge, experience or the content of their book. They know they know their stuff, but should they be putting themselves out there and telling the world that they think they have something important and useful to say?

Tara Halliday's explanation for this lingering apprehension is that cultural change moves at a much slower pace than societal change.

'For example, children learn from their parents at a very young age and they copy the gender roles that their parents learnt from their own parents. So a child, even a four-year-old today, is learning something that was taught two generations ago. Attitudes and behaviours are carried along unconsciously as well as consciously.

There have been great strides made in education, in emotional and in stress management; all sorts of things are happening and it's absolutely wonderful. But the fact is that we are trained at a young age in the values from two generations ago. If you go back over three generations, that doesn't really matter, because the values and attitudes remained the same over that timeframe, but now, because our whole society is changing so rapidly, we're starting to notice it and ask, "How come we're still doing that?" So, the question isn't really, for me, why fewer women are stepping up and writing books – it's just a reflection of the cultural lag, and it will change, but it may take time.'

Tara suggests that this is also why more women write about self-development, people management, coaching, communication and emotional subjects, while more men write about business processes and practices, technical and structural subjects. The genders still feel more comfortable in their own traditional realm, and currently the male viewpoint carries more authority than the female.

She pointed out that:

'We teach little boys that it's not OK to have emotions, it's not OK to show their feelings. We've got this nice phrase now, "Man up", which means that it's not OK for them to show their emotions, so where can they express themselves? Well, they can express themselves in facts and figures and technology. It's OK for a guy to geek out on his electronics, but it's not OK for him to walk into the office one morning with tears in his eyes and say, "I'm having a hard day today". Whereas a woman could do that and probably have a few women around her, patting her on the shoulder and asking, "Are you OK? Can I get you a cup of tea?" My personal view is that societies take a long time to change in terms of our emotional expression, and this is reflected in how men and women feel about writing their books and what they choose to write about.'

Cinderella

Cinderella struggles with too little money, too much housework and childcare, and finds it hard to make inroads at the networking ball.

The second area that the ABOO Circle's comments showed was a barrier to writing was the interrelated factors of time and money:

'Lack of adequate income and time to do it.'

'Finding it impossible to find the time without an external deadline (such as the publisher gave me). Meaning I had then to borrow some money to live on while I wrote it.'

'It was really the financial consideration of would this work? And would it ultimately be useful to me and my business goals?'

'Time – linked to being a mum and business owner.'

An author who has a particular relationship with time is Jane Duncan Rogers. Her husband, who was twelve years older than her, was diagnosed with cancer in 2010 at the age of sixty-five and only had a year to live. Jane was a life and small business coach and had been writing a blog for some time. She wrote about her husband's final year and eventually self-published her first book, *Gifted By Grief: A True Story of Cancer, Loss and Rebirth.* It's a very personal book about a unique story, but is full of nuggets of universally applicable information.

Jane's readers reacted especially positively to the chapter in which she shared the questions that she had asked her husband before he died: a list of practical things that a friend had insisted Jane get answered. These wide-ranging and hard-hitting questions included, 'What kind of coffin do you want? How do you want your body to be dressed? What are your passwords? What do you want done with your special, precious things that are not of monetary value, but that you would want someone to have?' Jane describes in her book the wonderfully bonding and happy morning she and her husband had when they eventually sat down and went through the questions. In response to her readers' requests, she put together a workshop, which was oversubscribed.

Next Jane created a workbook of the questions, and before she had even planned it, the whole thing turned in a social enterprise called Before I Go Solutions. Jane mentioned the idea of a book to a publisher she was introduced to, who commissioned with a short deadline.

Before I Go: The Essential Guide to Creating a Good End of Life Plan was written in two to three months, and Jane had to take time off work to write it, something she wouldn't have been able to do had it not been for the generosity of a friend.

> 'I knew I couldn't do it in the timeline that was required by the publisher unless I could focus properly on it. I knew that from my previous experience of writing, and I also knew roughly how much money it might take.
>
> I was just chatting to a friend about this one day and she said, "I'll lend you the money." She didn't need to be paid back for a while, so we set up a proper agreement and everything, but that really bought me the freedom just to be able to live and not have to think about doing any of the rest of the work that I was doing. I feel very grateful for that.'

Other women authors, though, struggle to take the time out from fee-earning work, especially if they are working part time, to write their book; yet others have to find time around the demands of family and domestic responsibilities; and some of course need to find a way through all of these in order to write.

> 'We usually have a ton of work to do, because we might have family commitments or lots of other jobs around the work that we do that typically fall to us, which take up our time. So we have an issue with making ourselves more visible, because that can be more risky, you can be more targeted. And then, also, we have the whole time considerations: the practicality of "What am I going to give up in order to do this?" And, for me, writing the book, it was a sacrifice on family time.'
>
> **Jane Frankland, author *IN Security***

Women-run businesses have a lower turnover than those with men in the lead. In 2016, 20% of small and medium-sized business (SME) employers and 22% of SMEs without employees in the UK were led by women (those controlled by a single woman or having a mainly women management team). Among SME employers, 20% of small and micro-businesses (with fewer than fifty employees) were led by women, compared to 15% of medium-sized businesses. Among SMEs with no employees, a lower proportion of businesses registered for VAT and/or PAYE were led by women (14%) compared to unregistered businesses (25%).[26]

---

26 'Women and the Economy' BRIEFING PAPER Number CBP06838, House of Commons Library, 9 March 2018

Daniel Priestley's entrepreneur accelerator programmes reflect these proportions:

> 'We have about 40% women on our Threshold Accelerator (for pre-VAT businesses), which is disproportionately high compared to overall figures of men- and women-led businesses. We have about 20–25% women on Key Person of Influence programmes, which is also disproportionately high given the number of women-led businesses at that level of turnover, but doesn't seem like it.'

These disparities in business growth mean more women may struggle to fund their own time and the financial investment in the publishing process than men. This is linked as both a cause and effect of the fact that women carry out an overall average of 60% more unpaid work than men, according to analysis by the Office of National Statistics.[27] The ONS worked with the ESRC Centre for Time Use Research, a world-leading multidisciplinary research group based in the University of Oxford's Department of Sociology with a team of researchers – including sociologists, economists, and demographers – who work with Time Use Data to investigate issues in areas including social life, work-life balance, family, gender, and economics.

---

27 https://www.ons.gov.uk/employmentandlabourmarket/
peopleinwork/earningsandworkinghours/articles/
womenshouldertheresponsibilityofunpaidwork/2016-11-10

'I do think the balance of responsibility of managing the home, kids, etc tends to fall on a woman's shoulders, so she just doesn't have enough time. And I think women focus more on getting stuff done, so probably we're doing more business and serving clients than finding time to write.'

The Office of National Statistics and ESRC Centre research showed that men averaged sixteen hours a week helping out at home, compared with twenty-six for women. Women aged twenty-six to thirty-five did the most unpaid work at thirty-four hours a week, while women on maternity leave averaged as much as sixty hours a week. The findings follow other recent research into the division of labour in the home.

Research by Oxfam in March 2018 concluded that UK women living with their partners spent an average of two working days a month more than men on housework and childcare.[28] Two Oxford University academics found, after analysing fifty years of data, that women do seventy-four minutes more housework a day than men – and that disagreements about housework are among the major sources of marital conflict.[29] (To be fair, men spend more time acting as unpaid transport, such as driving family members around, on DIY and taking the bins out.)

---

28   https://oxfamapps.org/media/press_release/2016-03-women-spend-two-days-a-month-more-than-men-on-housework-and-childcare/

29   https://www.demographic-research.org/volumes/vol35/16/35-16.pdf

The statistics also revealed that although the average amount of time parents devoted to childcare had fallen slightly since 2000, and despite declining support for traditional gender divisions of labour over the past thirty years, substantial support remains for women having the primary caring role for young children.

> 'While currently writing a book to a deadline, I've found myself distracted by the mess piling up around me. My cleaner has been off sick for a week and I live with a middle-aged man, two late-teenage girls and three dogs, none of whom are remotely bothered by, or feel responsible for, the mess. I don't have time to nag them or assign tasks, so as a typical woman author, I am pressing on and will deal with the fallout after the deadline, when normal service will be resumed. No humans or dogs were harmed in the writing of this book.'
>
> **Lucy McCarraher, author** *A Book of One's Own*

4

Many Hands, Many Minds

The Mentor

The Mentor is an experienced guide who can support even the most diffident author to produce a great and authoritative book.

Approximately one-fifth of the ABOO Circle said that a lack of mentors and supportive networks had been a barrier to them writing their book.

> 'This is why it matters so much that we shout about success stories and create powerful networks which support women on their journey, and mentoring is a great way of doing that.'[30]
> **Jessica Wilkinson, Petal & Co Founder**

The concept of a mentor comes from Homer's *The Odyssey*, where Mentor, a wise, old and caring man, looks after Telemachus, Odysseus' son. It started in 800 BC as a man-to-man relationship and still works most effectively, it seems, in predominantly male circles – public schools, universities, corporate culture and men's clubs. Although women have informally mentored each other within families and in the domestic sphere, it isn't embedded in our work relationships like it is for men, and is harder to find for women in the entrepreneurial space.

Alison Cork, founder of Make It Your Business, thinks that mentoring can help eliminate Impostor Syndrome:

> 'Women respond powerfully to other female mentors, as they are uniquely positioned to understand the particular practical and emotional challenges that face an aspiring entrepreneur.'[31]

---

30 *Mentoring Matters*, a project of the Female Founders Forum, March 2018

31 https://www.telegraph.co.uk/women/business/creating-role-models-mentors-key-female-entrepreneurship/

A mentor, formal or informal, can give you confidence through the book-writing process, and a published author can provide a supportive role model. The ABOO Circle are acting as mentors for you here, and other places beyond the book.

The fact is, there are some influential professional writing and publishing mentors in the business arena, and a bit of online research will find them. In Part Three, I go into detail about how to work with a professional mentor to create an excellent book.

Who's afraid of networking?

A recent study published in *Human Relations* has concluded that women build less effective networks than men because we under-estimate our worth (is this starting to sound familiar?).[32] While there is some element of exclusion by men, we also impose our own barriers to successful networking by being hesitant and having 'gendered modesty'. It seems we feel uncomfortable 'exploiting' social connections, which stops us benefiting from networking activities. In this study, women were shown to be careful not to over-capitalise on our connections, adding to the problem by underestimating and underselling our professional self-worth.

---

32 https://journals.sagepub.com/doi/abs/10.1177/0018726718804303?
   journalCode=huma

One interviewee said:

> 'Women look at networks from a social point of view…
> They do not ask the question "How will this benefit me?"
> Men, on the other hand, focus on the opposite, placing less
> emphasis on personal relationships, and make networking
> decisions for egoistic and instrumental motives.'

I personally find networking an uphill struggle if I'm not speaking at an event. Public speaking gives me a role and a way of 'selling' myself which offers other people value and doesn't sound boastful. As an introvert, I find both self-promotion and group conversation hard work in person, and much prefer one-to-one meetings and conversations, or written communications. I'm not sure whether this is also partly a woman thing.

> '… women are so suspicious of any interest that has not
> some obvious motive behind it, so terribly accustomed
> to concealment and suppression, that they are off at the
> flicker of an eye turned observingly in their direction.'
> **Virginia Woolf,** *A Room of One's Own*

Lyn Bromley and her co-author of *Trusted*, Donna Whitbrook, also talked about clients they had recently spoken with about their networking experience.

'We worked with two women who have both run their own businesses, both with very good backgrounds. They'd gone into a networking event, which was full of men. These are very credible women, but they could not get into the conversation; they couldn't step in; they kept themselves on the outskirts. And we were saying to them, "This is about going in and not taking control, but stepping in on that equal level." If we have that moment where we think, "Actually, we can't do this", we won't do it. Whereas, if we go in thinking, "What have we got to lose? I'm just going to go in anyway and do my thing", then we will confidently just go in and hold our own.'

This also led Lyn to recall a professional network opportunity of her own, which only became available to her after her book had been published – and perhaps because she'd never asked for it.

'My original career was an accountant, so I was in upper management. I actually contacted CIMA (Chartered Institute of Management Accountants) – because I've remained a member after all these years, even though I don't use it directly any longer – to ask if I could have a member spotlight article in the magazine to talk about the book and my background.

After the article was published, CIMA offered me a fast track to fellowship member. I'd never applied to be a fellow because I wasn't working directly in finance any longer, but when they saw that I'd written a book and read all of my career background, they invited me to be a fellow member.

Another man then said to me, "Oh, that's great, because there aren't many females that are fellows." I hadn't put myself forward, only because I wasn't working directly in that industry, but it may be that many women don't put themselves forward.'

In a recent survey for its 'Gender Diversity & Inclusion in Events Report',[33] the Bizzabo Blog found that, globally, more than two-thirds (69%) of all speakers were male, while less than one-third (31%) were female. Tech and finance events had the fewest women speakers, and the UK was ranked behind the US and Canada, with only 25% of our speakers across the board being female. Over the last three years there has been almost no progression on this globally. The causes are undoubtedly a combination of historic structural issues and market expectations, conscious and unconscious bias, and women's reluctance to put themselves forward for visibility and self-promotion.

The third main barrier to getting their own books written that the ABOO Circle referred to in their comments was the feeling of not having the tools to do the job:

'Not knowing how to do it.'

'I did not know about the tools and the structure.'

---

33   https://blog.bizzabo.com/event-gender-diversity-study

'Not knowing where to start, not being able to get beyond book idea to book content and reality, the day job, not being able to easily access the publishing world, working out how I could keep the IP [intellectual property]. Publishing looked like something only really clever and well-connected people got to do.'

I will address that issue in detail in Part Three, so no more to be said here.

Part Two

We Must Be Heroes

'Therefore I would ask you to write all kinds of books, hesitating at no subject however trivial or however vast.'

Virginia Woolf, *A Room of One's Own*

5

The Power Of The Printed Word

When I was twenty-one, I went to live in Australia. I expected to spend a couple of comparatively relaxing years finishing my degree in English and Drama, and maybe pursuing an acting career, but it didn't turn out like that. I started my first publishing company and became the Executive Editor of *Theatre Australia* magazine.

There was a good reason why no one had previously attempted to run a national performing arts magazine in a country the size of a continent with a tiny population: it was a commercial impossibility – and no one has managed it since. But for seven years we raised enough money from advertising, retail sales and subscriptions, and grants from national and state arts councils and other funding bodies, to produce eleven substantial issues a year, packed with articles and reviews by top theatre, film, opera and dance practitioners and writers.

It was relentlessly hard work – no sooner did one issue appear than the next one had to be pulled together, artwork and printing deadlines had to be met, contributors chased, copy edited, reviews and interviews written up, proofs read and re-read, contributors paid, subscribers' envelopes addressed and stuffed…

But most extraordinarily, it brought me an expert status out of all proportion to my actual expertise. When *Theatre Australia* launched, I was a young British student who had been in Australia about seven months; within a few more months, I had become a high-profile 'authority' on Australian performing arts, with an extensive network of and entrée to arts luminaries, supporters and investors, and was getting written about in, and writing for, other newspapers and magazines.

Next, I was offered a regular slot as a reporter covering the performing arts on my local TV News, and within another year was hosting my own weekly arts and entertainment programme. I got to interview stars like Barry Humphries/Dame Edna Everage, who made a complete fool of me on screen but was a charming house guest, and a very young Mel Gibson playing Hamlet in his first professional acting role. Mel was so shy, he only responded to my questions in grunts and monosyllables, and I had to invent some intelligent thoughts for him when I wrote up his interview for the magazine.

That was my first taste of the power of the printed word and what it can do for your authority and your profile. There's an influence and a legacy in published work that no other medium gives. If we'd started *Theatre Australia* more recently, we would probably have made it an online magazine, website or blog – and at the very least the production process would have been digital and so much simpler. But in a way, I'm glad that old school print was the only option then. No videos of my TV show or reviews exist anymore (probably for the best!), but all seventy-plus issues of *Theatre Australia* are stored in the archive of the Australian National Library, and a number of other university libraries.

Becoming an author

A couple of career moves and a good few years later, a publisher approached a colleague and me, first to write *The Work-Life Manual* for organisations, followed by a self-help book called *The Book of Balanced Living*. We wrote the business version together, then I volunteered to write the personal version. It turned out that the publisher had decided what they wanted the book to cover, handed me a contents page and expected me to go away and write the book. Which I did, creating case studies and exercises, tables and models to illustrate the text, and ending with guidelines for setting up your own business.

From being a respected but definitely backroom researcher in the then emerging area of work-life balance, and despite a strong dose of Impostor Syndrome, I became a senior consultant, hired by traditional blue chip companies, cool corporates like Virgin and Microsoft, big banks and legal firms, government departments and local councils, the NHS, and a wide range of SMEs. I advised policy makers in central government, set benchmarks and judged awards. The power of the printed word had shown itself again, and while these first books were not my best books, they revived my enthusiasm for writing and publishing, and what it could do for a business and a career.

Being a published author brings respect from the market you are writing for, and more broadly in the eyes of the world. In simple numerical terms, currently more men than women are gaining respect by writing business books – and there is a societal and cultural need for increased respect for women. One significant way of contributing to an increased respect for women in general is for more individual women to publish their books.

Coach Michele Attias, whose book is titled *Look Inside – Stop Seeking Start Living*, describes how writing her book challenged her professional, personal and cultural perceptions of herself and women in general.

'After years of being a writing contributor for online publications, publishing my book was one of the most empowering actions I could have taken. It made me into an authority in my field, and it opened up a platform of TV interviews, media features and invitations to give talks internationally. It increased my confidence and self-esteem when publishing my thoughts, expertise, experience, ideas and letting go of being judged. It gave me an extra platform, and it was wonderful to be contacted by readers who hired me to work as their life coach once they had finished reading my book.

I felt totally out on a limb and out of my comfort zone on the publishing journey, but I was helped along every step of the way. As a woman from a small town in the South of Spain, I didn't believe that this was possible for me. I had been brought up in a culture where women are more involved in bringing up children, and although this is an incredible job and hugely important, I wanted more. I had to shift my mindset and allow for the possibility that I was capable not only of publishing a book, but marketing and encouraging people to buy it. As a woman, this has been a great lesson for my own daughters, who have stood alongside me in this journey, and have seen what is possible for them to achieve.'

6

Brainpower

Keiron Sparrowhawk is the Founder and CEO of MyCognition, the visionary organisation carrying out pioneering scientific research into optimising cognitive potential. Keiron's inspiration for MyCognition sprang from a desire to improve the quality of life for individuals with cognitive deficits due to conditions such as Alzheimer's and Parkinson's, but he soon realised there could also be a massively positive impact from enhancing cognitive function in both education and the workplace. So MyCognition is using its R&D (research and development) as the basis for designing, developing, and testing products that could both assess and improve cognition.

'We do this across all ages, particularly working in the education sector, occupational health, looking at mental health within the workplace and mental health within the community. Not only do we look at psychiatric and neurological conditions, we also look at the impacts of poor cognition, poor mental health in areas such as diabetes, chronic pain, and other conditions.'

The author of *Executive Function – cognitive fitness for business*, a former neuroscientist and a successful entrepreneur, Keiron is also a board member of Dent Global. We were both on the judging panel of the Key Person of Influence PitchFest competition when I told him about *A Book of One's Own*. He offered to share MyCognition's recent and cutting-edge research, relevant to why fewer women than men start their own businesses or write their books.

Keiron's definition of cognition is that it represents all our thinking, all our thought processes, and all those thought processes that lead to our behaviour. The five domains of cognition are:

- *Processing Speed* – the speed and accuracy by which we put our thoughts into action;

- *Attention* – our ability to focus, divide our attention, give it to others, distribute our attention, be on the lookout for threats and things like that, or listening out;

- *Working Memory* is being able to retain a limited amount of information for a short time and retrieve and use it during this time, enabling us to solve problems and make decisions;

- *Episodic Memory* is our ability to recall past events that are relevant to current or future situations, effectively our 'wisdom'; and

- *Executive Function* is a set of cognitive processes that include planning, organising, being creative, self-regulation, decision-making, calculating and comprehending – the ability to strategically plan, act on the plan, change strategy if necessary and be in control of our emotions.

'With a weak Executive Function, we're more likely to get easily upset or angry, whereas when it's fit and healthy, we're less likely to get upset and angry.'

A key fact that has emerged from MyCognition's research is that *there is no significant difference in cognition, or any aspect of it, in general between women and men.* There is no way in which women could be considered, or we could label ourselves, as cognitively less able than or different to men. I would hope we all know that, but it's good to have the scientific research to back ourselves up.

The data for MyCognition's research comes from subjects as young as six and as old as 102, and it does show differences in certain domains across age ranges, in both men and women. Cognition increases from birth, it plateaus in the early twenties, and this plateau extends through into the fifties, when it begins to decline. Then we see a more rapid decline from sixty into older age, making it a bell-shaped curve, with a plateau at the top.

This is not good news for me – I was born in 1954 (like Oprah Winfrey, Angela Merkel, Annie Lennox, Carly Fiorina, Condoleezza Rice, Alice Kaplan and Cherie Booth), so I should be on the downward curve. It doesn't feel like it, though. If the principle of 'use it or lose it' is valid, I'm doing at least as much cognitive work as I've ever done, and feel like the breadth and depth of my experience feed into my Executive Function abilities to keep them running at as high a speed as ever. I'd like to think that activities like planning and writing books develop and sustain high levels of cognition.[34] Even my working memory doesn't seem to be in decline, though I admit to recently turning on both a hob ring and a tap, getting a sudden idea for this book, rushing off to make a note – and not going back to the kitchen for twenty minutes. Luckily my daughter went into the kitchen and headed off potential fire and flooding.

'What happened?' she asked when I got back, assuming I'd been called away to some emergency, and shaking her head in teenage scorn when I sheepishly said I'd just had rather a good idea.

The authors of a recent study in *Neuropsychology*[35] also conclude that:

> 'The influences of demographic factors on late-life cognition may be reflective of broader socioeconomic factors, such as educational opportunity and related differences in physical and mental activity across the life span.'

There's no question that I've been lucky on those fronts.

---

34   https://www.nia.nih.gov/health/cognitive-health-and-older-adults

35   Paul W. H. Brewster, Rebecca J. Melrose, María J. Marquine, Julene K. Johnson, Anna Napoles, Anna MacKay-Brandt, Sarah Farias, Bruce Reed, Dan Mungas. *'Life Experience and Demographic Influences on Cognitive Function in Older Adults'. Neuropsychology*, 2014

Keiron's research shows that in the younger years, overall the cognition of girls moves ahead faster than that of boys. And adolescence, which has a slowing effect on the developing cognition of both genders, slows down the positive increase in boys more than it does for girls. So, if we girls felt that we were more mature in our teens and early twenties than boys of our own age, we were right.

'In terms of getting on, and in terms of having the cognitive capacity to do anything, because cognition controls not only our thinking, but our behaviour and everything else, women are ahead at that stage. So, women are capable of doing whatever men can do, and in some instances, you could certainly argue women are more capable than men. In terms of business – starting businesses, running a business, writing books, all of that – there should be nothing to hold women back. Nothing at all.'

But having enjoyed faster maturity when we were young – and here's the kicker – when we get to our fifties, women's cognition starts to decline more quickly than men's. Keiron Sparrowhawk offers a possible solution:

'Now, we've got no evidence at the moment to suggest it's down to something like the menopause, but that's what we're speculating is causing that post-fifty faster decline in women's cognition than in men's. Again, this is based on conjecture. I have no evidence, but it seems likely that HRT would go a long way to alleviating that decline; it could actually build cognitive resilience. I think part of the reason that we're seeing this cognitive decline as women enter the menopause is because there's been a negative bias against HRT, because its cardiovascular side effects were probably over-hyped some years back. And I think health professionals have got to look from the point of view of what's the risk benefit overall. They should take cognition into account in women's overall quality of life. And women too should be thinking of this as a health aspect when they consider whether or not to take HRT.'

If the hormones of male adolescence affect cognition (think lack of emotional control, risky behaviour), then it seems logical that the hormones that produce mood swings and the red mist anger that some of us experience, along with hot flushes and night sweats, would also be connected with an interruption to the Executive Function. Having said that, I've co-founded and developed Rethink Press, founded the Business Book Awards and written ten of my twelve books since I turned fifty, so I'm not prepared to accept that my cognition has been overly compromised by age.

Keiron Sparrowhawk points out that though there is no difference in general in the cognitive abilities of women and men, there are clear differences in behaviour and attitudes; differences that should be celebrated and exploited for the good outcomes that diversity brings.

'We know that if you've got a board on a company that's made up of middle-aged white males, it's more likely to fail than if it's diverse in terms of culture, age and gender.'

He believes such differences are produced partly through our culture in which women are still informed, covertly if not overtly, that they should be in second place behind men, and partly by differences within the hormones of men and women, particularly at specific times of life. His research around the area of cortisol, the hormone produced by stress, shows that within the population there is a group of people who over-respond to cortisol, and more of these are men.

Men's over-response to cortisol often leads them to behave in ways that can either be classed as heroic, strong, well-meaning, or be classed as inappropriate, wrong and even criminal. On the spectrum of responses to stress, to a cortisol rush, we see more men pushing themselves further on to the 'good' end, in terms of doing wonderful extreme acts that impress, and also into the very 'bad' end of behaviour, than women. So, although women do respond to the release of this transmitter stress hormone, their responses form a slimmer bell curve of extreme reaction than men's.

From an evolutionary point of view, Keiron suggests that back in the days when we were small nomadic tribes, under threat of attack by wild animals or other tribes, this over-reaction to cortisol meant the people who were first into the fray were the people most likely either to die for the good of the tribe, or to return victorious – in both cases, they would be able to view themselves, and be seen by others, as heroes. And these would most likely be men, as women would be doing the equally valuable but less obviously 'heroic' role of guarding the camp and protecting the children.

> 'If you bring that behaviour and attitude forward to today, you have more men volunteering for the armed services – think of the first world war, when working men felt they were signing up for adventure or death in the service of king and country. "I can come back a hero or die for my country. I have nothing to lose" is the male response to cortisol, unlike women who feel responsible for their children, homes and more vulnerable within our society.'

Keiron believes that the male 'heroic' risk-taking mindset also shows itself today in relation to activities like starting businesses and writing books – activities where you do expose yourself to risk.

> 'Men think, "I'm happy to do that, regardless of what I've achieved or the skills I have… what have I got to lose? I could be a hero." Despite the fact that women have got just as good, or better, experience, and as good or higher levels of skills, they're still feeling in protective, defensive rather than attacking mode.'

Dr Tara Halliday, author of *Unmasking*, a book about Impostor Syndrome, agrees.

'Part of the Impostor Syndrome research shows that men are more likely to say they're certain about something when they're 70% certain, whereas a woman would have to wait until she's 95% certain to say she's certain about it. So, in supporting women in writing books, we need to help them discover their own authority that they don't see themselves. This is generational: we were taught effectively from our grandmother's perspective that a woman can't say, "I'm an expert on this". "Who am I to be doing this?" is the song of Impostor Syndrome.'

Even if it goes against the cultural – and even hormonal – grain, women must learn to be heroes too; to take more risks, or realise the risks are not that great, and be confident in knowing that they have the experience, skills and knowledge to put themselves out there and nothing bad is going to happen. The children are going to survive, and the camp will stay standing.

Keiron Sparrowhawk tells us bluntly:

'We have to begin to emphasise to women of all ages that, listen, you are at least as good as men, so put yourselves forward. If you don't put yourselves forward, you're leaving a vacuum into which some half-witted man can fall and take that position, whether it's a job or a position of authority or being the author of a book, that you should be holding.'

With the worst kinds of disrespect for women abroad in society, we can make a difference. We know that books bring respect to their authors, and more books by women add to the total sum of respect for women more widely. For this reason, as well as the others I and the ABOO Circle are about to give you, we must stop feeling like impostors, step forward as heroes, and write our books.

The Hero

The Hero has overcome her challenges to achieve her goal, and continues to make her book her weapon and shield in the campaign for influence.

7

Reasons To Write Your Book

'It would be a thousand pities if women wrote like men, or lived like men, or looked like men, for if two sexes are quite inadequate, considering the vastness and variety of the world, how should we manage with one only?'
Virginia Woolf, *A Room of One's Own*

I asked our ABOO Circle of over fifty women authors:

'Has publishing your book(s) been useful to your business or professional standing?'

- Not one author said their book had been *'Not useful at all'*

- Two authors (4%) said their book had been *'Not so useful'*

- Five women (11%) replied that their book had been *'Somewhat useful'*

- Fifteen (31%) reported that their book had been *'Very useful'*

- But over half – twenty-six women authors and 54% – reported that their book had been *'Extremely Useful'* to their business or professional standing

'Our book was published ten months ago. Opportunities have presented themselves and doors have been opened as a result of writing *Trusted*. We have spoken on national and international platforms, secured new clients and identified other opportunities following publication. We were both confident women before we'd written a single word, but we are noticeably more confident now, which was an unexpected outcome.'

Lyn Bromley and Donna Whitbrook, authors *Trusted*

More specifically, I asked:

'What benefits has publishing your book(s) brought you and your business?'

These questions were not, of course, mutually exclusive, so most ABOO authors ticked several boxes.

- Sixteen women (34%) said their book had given them the *'Ability to raise my fees'*

- Twenty-two authors (47%) said they had increased *'Contact with key people in my industry'*

- Thirty-one (66%) told me that their book had brought them *'Influence in my industry or market'*

- Thirty-four (75%) replied that they had increased their *'Prospects and clients'*

- Thirty-six (77%) had gained *'Speaking gigs and other public platforms'* as a result of writing their book

- Thirty-eight (81%) ABOO authors found that their book had brought them *'Authority as an expert in my field'*

- Additionally, eleven ABOO authors (27%) said their books had brought them *'Benefits I couldn't have imagined'*.

> 'I've been asked to be columnist for an internationally acclaimed online industry magazine, *WWD*. I'm totally amazed that I've unpacked a new skill. I could never have imagined that I could be paid to write. Incredible!'

One mature author wrote:

> 'Before my book has even been published, writing it and talking about it has opened up my world in ways I could never have imagined. Best of all, absolutely unbelievably off the scale best of all, is that it's given me the confidence I have been seeking all my life! It might have taken some time and tears, but it forced me to articulate what I stand for.'

When they told me more about what benefits their books had brought them, the ABOO Circle used words and phrases like:

Reason #1 – clarity and confidence

Every author I work with finds that the process of planning and writing their books is both personally and professionally illuminating. Organising your thoughts, knowledge, experience and expertise into a detailed configuration – the blueprint of a logical and enlightening journey for your reader – can be a hard exercise, but it is always highly rewarding. It forces you to interrogate the steps of your process, your client or customer journey, and the way you want to present your practice and your data to your readers.

> 'The very process of writing the book is valuable in itself: self-affirming and confidence-boosting. Do it for that aspect alone!'

Writing the manuscript through several iterations then gives you the opportunity to unpack and review everything, from the currency of your views to the whole premise of your business. The book-writing process has triggered a considerable number of entrepreneur authors into re-positioning or pivoting their businesses – for the better and often the bigger.

Audrey Chapman, author of *Love Selling,* gives an honest insight into the effect that writing her book had on her.

> 'I firmly believe that the time is now for women to stand up and be counted. Opportunity is out there for everyone, so long as we're clear on the outcome we want and prepared to do the work required.
>
> My own publishing/writing journey has been part business focused and part healing. When I decided to write my book, I never expected that to be so. Firstly, having to focus and be fully present with what I wanted to say and what I wanted to share via my writing made me literally review every aspect of who I believed I was and what I believed I had to offer. It turned out to be a pretty intense healing journey for me, and my business eventually took off financially as a result of this process.

I think writing the book – and I've spoken to other authors as your book makes you part of a network of authors – is actually quite an experience. Although you write the book for commercial reasons, you actually find that it's a real introspection; you start to reflect on yourself and what it is that you want to say. If you have created this opportunity to have a voice, what are you going to say? Because there's quite a responsibility that goes with that.'

Having written your manuscript – even if no one else ever reads it – can bring a new level of confidence in a wide range of situations. Your book is probably the most extended piece of writing you will do. It creates an archive of content that you can re-purpose into blog posts, articles, podcasts, workshops, courses, presentations and keynote speeches, saving you time and assuring you that whatever format you deploy your edited book manuscript in, it will be the most eloquent and articulate formulation of your knowledge.

'Personal growth and self-esteem. A confidence in my capacity to meet challenge. A personal joy and satisfaction when I hear from women who have been helped and supported through my work, globally!'

What's more, pitching, presenting, speaking and training all become easy, or easier, when you've written your book. Through the writing process, through formulating your thoughts into sharp headings, coherent sentences and flowing paragraphs; illustrating them with appropriate and well-formed case studies and anecdotes; using your own story to underpin your learning journey; and accumulating supporting research and data, you save all this content to the cloud drive in your head and can easily recall and present it in the appropriate situation. A note or a heading on a PowerPoint slide is enough to trigger the section or story you wrote in your book in familiar, speakable phrases. A question from the audience or a roomful of decision-makers is fluently answered from the process you laid out in the book.

> 'I wasn't aware that I wasn't standing in my truth, but being faced with actually documenting or sharing what I believed that I had to offer all of a sudden made me really sit up and consider whether I was saying what I meant. Don't say what others want you to say; say what you mean. And that's what I did, and it's given me a huge sort of internal confidence.'
>
> **Audrey Chapman, author *Love Selling***

Even if you are someone who speaks more fluently than you write, you will still have ordered your material more logically and methodically on the page. I'm an experienced speaker, but sometimes I honestly don't know what I think until I've physically typed it and seen my ideas take shape in words on the screen – and then I have to clarify exactly what I mean by editing, cutting and pasting, using the thesaurus to find the precise words I want. Then I'm ready to speak.

Despite being an introvert, I've always enjoyed being on stage (it's a controllable space), but whether I'm acting or speaking, my worst fear has always been drying – forgetting what comes next or being unable to dredge up the answer to a question. The repetitive process of writing, editing, rewriting and proofreading a book means that the content is etched in my memory – I actually see in my mind the printed pages of, for instance, *The WRITER Process*, or the *Publish Pathway* when I'm speaking, or training a roomful of people on how to write or publish their books.

Jane Duncan Rogers, author of *When I Go,* puts it this way:

'Writing a book (and it can be recording and then getting it transcribed and edited) is crucial if you want to not only find your voice but shout your message loud and clear. Even in these days of video popularity, people respect the published written word in a way that brings increased credibility – and that brings confidence, which breeds more confidence to speak more often and more loudly about one's message. So, if you have the inkling to write a book – go for it!'

Reason #2 – authority and influence

'It has given me credibility: with clients, with the industry and with myself.'

When I was young, I was small, slim and pretty. Now, I'm… small. I used to wear lots of makeup and the highest heels. The heels led to foot operations and now I wear flats. And less makeup.

You might think I regret the passing of my younger self. I don't. What I have now is so much more valuable. I have authority – some of it has come with age and experience; more has come from being the author of twelve books.

We've all seen the statistics about the lack of women CEOs, women on boards, women in politics, women in power, the gender pay gap, gender inequality, and most of us have some experience of how that plays out in real life. One of the underlying reasons for all these issues is that women are not viewed as being authoritative. The default model of authority is still male. But there are a few things that confer authority in a gender-unbiased way, and one of those is being the author of a book.

Writing gives clarity, shape and form to your thoughts and ideas, which helps you express them succinctly and authoritatively in person. Writing also helps develop your 'voice', whether written or spoken, and a way to rehearse its style.

Everyone respects an author, even more than we might imagine. In the world of entrepreneurs it's common to talk about writing a book, and many business owners, coaches and consultants aim to do so. They take the first steps towards doing it, sometimes pay to go on courses, or get coaching to write their book – but those who actually finish writing their books and get them published are still a small, elite minority, which makes us all the more valued and authoritative.

The Federation of Small Businesses (FSB) spoke to 1,900 women business owners in the UK for a report[36] that found women-led businesses faced many of the same challenges all small firms encounter, but key challenges included balancing work and family life (40%), achieving credibility for the business (37%) and a lack of confidence (22%). Writing a book might not help address the first as you're writing it, but it definitely improves business credibility and confidence.

Helen Walbey, FSB Diversity Policy Chair, said:

'Understanding the importance of diversity and getting more women into business is critical for a dynamic and vibrant small business sector. That's why we need to work out what the barriers are for women and break them down one by one.'

---

36 Federation of Small Businesses report, 'Women in Enterprise: The Untapped Potential', 21 April 2016.

Many of the ABOO Circle commented on the authority their book has conferred on them:

> 'Being invited and sponsored to attend the Gibraltar Literary Festival with well-known authors, celebrities and journalists.'

> 'Respect and positive feedback – being shortlisted for the Business Book Awards was certainly something I didn't expect.'

> 'It's given me a platform that far exceeds my speciality in sales. I now enter into conversation with C-level and key influencers… although they don't necessarily talk specifically about me being an author, it's broadened the conversation immensely. I am now considered more as a businessperson who has a keen interest in sales. My engagement with clients has taken on a far more multi-dimensional approach and I'm now not just a salesperson.'

> 'It has been very important for me. In a world where men can still find it easier to be perceived as an authority (especially in some industries), we need to put our best foot forwards and use assets such as the book to help move our brands, reputations and businesses forward.'

> 'I think we all have credibility, but what it does, it sort of elevates you in your field. All of a sudden, you've written a book and people come and ask you your expert opinion on things. They want to know what you have to say about it;

they are seeking validation and guidance on the basis of the book. It positions you really credibly in terms of prospects and your existing clients.'

Reason #3 – prospects and clients

And, speaking of prospects and clients, the well-leveraged book is the best business card and marketing brochure combined, and pre-sells you and your services to your ideal clients. (I'll tell you how to make sure this happens in Part Three.)

Marianne Page, author of two books – *Process to Profit* and *Simple, Logical, Repeatable*, is an impressive example of this because she keeps count of the clients who sign up with her business as a direct result of having read one or both of her books, and the fees they pay her. And it's now running into hundreds of thousands of pounds.

She said:

'Writing your book is an empowering experience. Getting your thoughts, opinions and expertise down on paper is a massive confidence boost, particularly when you win your first piece of business from someone who has invested time and money in your book and wants to learn more from you as a result. Both of my books have had, and continue to have, a significant impact on my revenue, and have brought me an increasing number of opportunities to speak.'

As a high-level business coach, Sandra Webber has to pitch her services to HR Directors of large corporates, so she uses her book strategically, bringing it to interviews with her as a secret weapon. She finds that her book, *Own It*, has often done its work ahead of her in-person meetings.

> 'I had a job interview where, as I was leaving, the interviewer said, "Maybe we'll feature in your next book". I hadn't mentioned my writing at all during the interview, although it was on my CV. I think having a book helped me get the job as it shows I am competent in my subject matter. In my industry that is particularly important when I'm getting "screened" by HR Directors (often half my age) for coaching work with senior executives. Just dropping in "Have you read my book? This is the best way of getting to know the type of coach I am," is a powerful credibility tool. It's almost like a trump card – and sometimes someone will say, "Oh, I've always wanted to write a book, but never done it".'

Audrey Chapman talks about 'significance' rather than 'authority', which gives a slightly different perspective, but still results in clients and income.

> 'Without a doubt, writing *Love Selling* gave me a new level of significance. And I don't use that word lightly. Significance in terms of being able to introduce myself; people add weight to the fact that you're an author. It's not

something that everybody does, and it's definitely given me opportunities, and business has come directly to me as a result of the book. One client in particular, a very significant client, only found me because of the book and they signed up to a contract for the best part of £100,000 literally ten minutes into our first meeting.

The reader has an insight into who you are, they pick up your personality and whether that sits with their organisation. So, absolutely, it's had a profound effect. And it's funny because when it came out, my fixation was still on how many books were going to sell, as opposed to what would come in as a result of the book. And then that one book, just that one book, generated all of that business, and, in fact, has rippled out because the former Chief Finance Officer of that particular organisation has now become a personal client since leaving that business.'

Reason #4 – speaking and platforms

If you would love to get more or better paid or higher profile speaking engagements, then writing and publishing your book will help you achieve this aim. Every day, we see experts and pundits appearing in the media, and almost inevitably they're introduced as 'the author of… ' Their book is the source of their authority to comment on their specialist subject. Not only does their book define their expertise, but it's very likely how the programme producer or journalist found them in the first place.

Amazon is one of the most powerful search engines, and if you have a book published on Amazon and someone searches your name, your book title, or key words in the description of your book, Amazon's algorithm ensures that you and your book will appear at the top of the search page.

Your area of expertise may not be of interest to the media (although it's likely that your local radio station and newspaper will love to interview you as a local author), but your own industry will definitely be interested in getting you to speak, take part in panel discussions or run workshops, at home and potentially all over the world. But you need to be pro-active in finding the decision-makers and getting your book out to them.

Monica Or has written three books over four year on her niche in the hospitality industry. Her books cover all aspects of customer service: *Star Quality Hospitality – The Key to a Successful Hospitality Business; Star Quality Experience – The Hotelier's Guide to Creating Memorable Guest Journeys; and Star Quality Talent – Inspiring Hospitality Careers.* She has consistently leveraged them to raise her profile and become the go-to expert in her field.

'From having my books published I have been invited to speak abroad at conferences, flown business class, accommodation and expenses paid for as well as a speaker fee and large book orders. I have been paid to work with partners to run a Thought Leaders workshop, webinar and white paper. Content from my book has been turned into online courses. My status with my industry peers has been elevated and they now take me much more seriously. I have been interviewed for trade magazines and spoken at many conferences. It is now a lot easier to connect with people in my industry: many CEOs and Managing Directors are happy to meet with me and I can contact them directly without having to get past their gatekeepers!

Once your book is published, don't be shy, shout about it. Share your knowledge far and wide.'

In a very different niche, Vicki Wusche has also assiduously published an ongoing series of books, regularly updated, about investing in property (*Using Other People's Money: How to invest in property; Make More Money from Property: From investor thinking to a business mindset; Property for the Next Generation; The New Estate: Insights from the 22nd Century*), the latest of which is *The Wealthy Retirement Plan*. She too has worked hard at using her book to position herself in her industry.

'It certainly brought me speaking events. When I first started to write I was focused purely on property investing – a very male-dominated environment, there weren't a lot of females around. I had my eye on one event that I really wanted to speak at, so I just hammered away, constantly going to events, and I always used to carry a book in my hand and three in my bag in case anybody ever mentioned it. In the audience there are always other event hosts, and I found I easily got speaking events.

This gives you the opportunity to speak above and beyond and around the book. Because what you write in the book is what you think at that moment when it finally goes to print, but your understanding evolves. Now the content from my books has been repurposed into articles for the press, for online courses and live events and speaking opportunities. I have spoken all over the county and abroad, not just about property investing, but at inspiring women events and business events. Your book is a reserve of material that you can speak about in many forms.'

Jane Frankland has also used her book to position herself in the male-dominated industry of cybersecurity. In fact, her book is starting to turn the industry upside down in terms of gender awareness: as I've already said, that is precisely the subject of *IN Security – Why a Failure to Attract and Retain Women in Cybersecurity is Making Us All Less Safe.* She is now a sought-after speaker all over the world, distilling the message of her book and leading campaigns for better practice in her industry.

'I was being asked to speak more because I had raised my visibility. I was already very active on social media, I was already writing blogs and doing videos, but when I committed to write the book and I started posting about it, I immediately gained speaking events. Because there are low numbers of women in the industry, I was then quite attractive to event organisers who wanted to be represented by more women. So, I literally said yes to every single opportunity.

Most of them scared me, so I just had a deal with myself. I would say yes immediately, then I kind of silently screamed in the background, and then prepared for it and got on with it.

Over the years, I did so many free speaking events, and because, when I was talking, when I was keynoting or on a panel, I was received really well, I started to get more paid events. I then made a decision that I'd done enough time with free events to actually start charging, and then to only accept paid speaking events.

So, once I said no to the first unpaid one, the others became easier and, interestingly, what then happened was I got a ton of paid speaking almost overnight.'

These three ABOO authors really have taken up the challenge to write their books and leverage them to create platforms for themselves, positioning themselves as women experts in their industries. They are all heroes, sharing their experience and making a difference.

Reason #5 – book magic

Confidence, authority, influence, clients, income and speaking platforms are all massively positive outcomes from writing and publishing your book. From the experience of mentoring and publishing hundreds of entrepreneur authors' business books, I recognise that these are all predictable results. Of course, you can publish your book and tell no one and do nothing with it, and perhaps the effect will be low, but if you follow the suggestions for promotion in the next section, and think creatively about how you can use your book to achieve your goals, all of the above are entirely predictable.

But there are always some unpredictable results to publishing a book of one's own – sometimes seeming almost magical. Some have found their book has put them in touch with their own heroes; others have been invited onto government committees, or unexpectedly doubled their business, or…

Joy Zarine, author of *The Five Star Formula*, talks about her version of book magic.

'Writing my book felt cathartic for me. For so many years I have had ideas bubbling away inside of me, but it was only when writing them down – giving them space to grow and evolve on paper – that they not only became clearer but also more powerful.

Publishing my book felt far more challenging. The process was no longer about getting ideas out of my head and onto paper, but instead was about sharing those ideas with the world. What would people think of my ideas; what would they think of me? Did I have the right to give my opinion, and more importantly, did my ideas and opinions even matter to anyone else?

Accepting that I might be putting myself in the firing line for criticism was difficult, but it was only when a client of mine said, "In one hundred years you'll be dead anyway. The world, our industry, needs to know what you have to say. So stop being scared and just publish the damn book." He was right. I was the only person standing in my own way. And so with a deep breath, in a moment of bravery, I agreed to press "publish".

From that day to today, I cannot tell you the number of people who have contacted me, telling me that my book had changed their lives. Changed the way in which they saw their business; how they worked with people; how they served their customers better in a more authentic way than ever before. People who were reading my book were scaling their businesses, winning awards and even selling their businesses. All thanks to advice from me.

People in countries I have never visited write to me and thank me for writing the book. But beyond these stories, people are in tune with who I am and what I am about before they have even met me. People know from reading my book if I am the right person to help them with their business, and maybe they also know if I am not – which helps save time as well!

Writing a book won't change your life. Publishing a book can do, and publishing a book about your passion for your industry almost certainly will do.'

Perhaps there's a way in which, as women, our lower confidence in our abilities to write and publish our books makes the magic of making a difference even more powerful when it happens. However, I wouldn't want the fact that we perhaps feel more special in our achievements because we are thinner on the ground than our male counterparts to stop us encouraging other women to equalise the numbers. In fact, every single one of the ABOO Circle was desperate to encourage other women to write their books.

Tara Halliday, author of *Unmasking:*

'I would say the first thing to encourage women to write a book would be to focus on the gift that she's giving to others; the wisdom and the experience and the insights that she's passing on. And to emphasise the fact that her personal story is important. It can be instructional, it can be inspirational, even if she doesn't think it is.

I think it's important for more women to write books and raise their profiles as the experts they are. We have a tendency not to promote the important things we do, which is a shame for future generations of female business leaders.'

Vicki Wusche, author of *The Wealthy Retirement Plan*, told me:

'Every time I hesitate, every time I don't sell, every time I don't finish a book, every time I don't write a blog... If I feel that I know something that, if I shared it with you, could help you in some way, why wouldn't I do that? And I think if more women start thinking around their content in that way, that they know something that could help someone else that would also – I hate to bring it back to the female psyche, but I think that would trigger a woman more, maybe, than a man.'

Alison Jones, of Practical Inspiration Publishing and author of *This Book Means Business*, makes this point:

'I think it's really important that we have more women writing business books, because I think that is the only thing that will ultimately change the culture: when it becomes more normal, when it becomes impossible to ignore the fact that half the books on the shelf are by women. And I think it's important that they are writing more and more books that are skills-based and general, partly because those are the books that men are going to read too.'

Daniel Priestley of Dent Global and the Key Person of Influence programme makes these recommendations:

> 'We need to make sure that women understand that writing and publishing a book is a certain way of advancing their business success rate; that it supports an entrepreneur to be able to work fewer hours and have more freedom and flexibility, if that's what they want to do, by raising their prices and generating leads.'

The long view

I was lucky enough to grow up with a hero. My mother, Gillian Wagner, at the age of fifty-one turned herself into the writer she'd always wanted to be.

In 1978, she became Chair of Barnardo's at the same time as the children's charity appointed its first woman Chief Executive. The men on the committee were openly worried about having two women in the most senior positions, but of course it was fine. Mum also got Princess Diana to become the Patron when Princess Margaret got bored of the job and resigned.

She recalls:

> 'I suddenly found myself racing up the ladder and about to be appointed to a position of great responsibility, and I thought, "I know nothing! I must get myself qualified

somehow." So, I went to the London School of Economics (the LSE) and took a Diploma in Social Administration.

I think it may well be right that women are more aware of the gaps in their capabilities than are men. When I saw this promotion coming, I thought, "Well, yes, OK, go for it, but do at least try to know what you are talking about".'

Later, after discovering the extraordinary archive of records and letters stored at Barnardo's, Gillian decided she would write a thoroughly researched biography of the founder, Dr Barnardo. She was worried that people would think that, as she was Chair of the organisation and a woman, it would be another uncritical hagiography of 'the great man'. So she decided she would get academic credentials in place before writing the book, and enrolled with the LSE to write a PhD on 'Dr Barnardo and the Charity Organisation Society – a reassessment of the Arbitration Case of 1877'. This felt like a big risk in itself as, if she didn't achieve it, the whole organisation would know she had failed. But she got the PhD, wrote the book and finally, in 1979, Weidenfeld and Nicholson published *Barnardo*.

More books followed. *Children of the Empire* told the stories, mostly sad and many in their own words from the letters they sent back, of the British children who were 'saved' by charities like Barnardo's in the nineteenth century and (often illegally) sent to Australia, New Zealand, Canada and America (the Empire), right up to children evacuated overseas in the Second World War.

'Of all my books, my favourite is the one I wrote about the children who were sent overseas, *Children of the Empire.* Some of the children, who of course were adults and quite old by that stage, got in contact with me to say that I was the first person who had realised their total desolation, what it felt like to be sent overseas as such a small child.'

After chairing Barnardo's, Gillian became Chair of the Thomas Coram Foundation and wrote a book about his life, too – *Thomas Coram, Gent.*

'Thomas Coram is my greatest hero; he was a feminist before his time. He got aristocratic ladies to support the Foundling Hospital. Men wouldn't, because they thought it would encourage depravity, but Coram persuaded their wives to back the hospital, and they exerted a quiet but very real power over their husbands to bring them round to the cause.'

Then came the wonderfully titled *The Chocolate Conscience* – the stories of the Quaker Rowntree, Cadbury and Fry families, their incredibly successful chocolate businesses, and the clash between their moral values and commercial reality. And most recently, *Miss Palmer's Diary: The Secret Journals of a Victorian Lady* was launched in 2017 just after Gillian's ninetieth birthday. It's the story of her great grandmother, Ellen Palmer, based on the daily diaries she kept from 1847 when aged seventeen.

'I've always fought for a greater respect for women in the charity sector, government and the finance world I found myself in, and becoming an author definitely gave me a more serious profile.'

Go forth and write

There is a predictably unpredictable magic to writing and publishing a good book. Every author whose book I've published comes back to me at some point with a story that usually opens with, 'You won't believe what's happened… ' and ends with '… and it's all because of the book.'

The key phrase, though, is 'a good book', and the way to ensure your book presents you to your market and the world in the best and most professional way is to work with a book mentor. If you have a business book that you know you should write, especially if it's your first, do yourself and your readers a favour and work with a mentor to get it planned and written.

It's time for us to step up, write our books, tell our stories and be heroes to the world, our gender, our market and our daughters. In the next section, I'll tell you exactly how to create the right mindset, then plan, write and publish your book in the least stressful and time-consuming way possible.

Part Three

Kill Your Angel, Write Your Book

'She was intensely sympathetic. She was immensely charming. She was utterly unselfish. She excelled in the difficult arts of family life. She sacrificed herself daily... Killing the Angel in the House was part of the occupation of the woman writer.'

Virginia Woolf, 'Professions for Women', *The Death of the Moth and Other Essays*

8

The Angel, The Librarian
And Miss Moneypenny

The Angel

The Angel is the siren call of what your grandmother or
even your mother may have considered the pure spirit
of womanhood.

Let me introduce you to three more archetypes, one of whom might hinder and two who could help you get your book written.

The first is a 'phantom' brought to life in Virginia Woolf's 1931 talk 'Professions for Women', later published in her collection, *The Death of the Moth and Other Essays*. Almost ninety years later, most women will recognise 'The Angel in the House': she is the idealised daughter, sister, wife, partner, mother, colleague, manager… who, whatever age you are, will be lurking in your subconscious, sweet and smiling, ready to sabotage your book by reminding you that real women put the needs of others first, they feel the pain of others almost more than their own, and they sacrifice themselves to take that pain away and make others happy.

The Angel will also helpfully remind you that as a woman, your own views should come second to those of others, and even in the unlikely case that you do have something clever or original to say, it's selfish to step into the limelight when someone else, possibly a man, would take pleasure in being praised for presenting such ideas as their own.

Perhaps, if you're very young, you may think you don't have an Angel of your own, or that if you do, she's a shadowy phantom who won't bother you unduly when you've decided to write your book. The more mature among us may believe we've subdued our Angel in previous battles. Beware. The Angel in the House is a powerful creature, with an arsenal of subtle and sneaky tactics, and a Narnia-sized wardrobe of disguises (sometimes as your mother). Before you start writing, it's best to bring her into the light of day and face her with the facts.

You could thank her for her care – after all, she's only trying to protect you from making a fool of yourself in a man's world, and neglecting your womanly duties – before telling her in no uncertain terms that you *are* writing your book, and that while you are doing so, you will not be needing her advice. If she refuses your offer of early retirement, you could try visualising leading her into bright sunlight and watching her fade into nothing, or setting her up with a comfortable sofa, a subscription to Netflix and six months' supply of gin and tonic.

I was about eight when I read E Nesbit's *Five Children and It*. From the immersive world of the early 20th Century summer, where the family of five children discover the sand fairy Psammead and his seductive wishes, I picked up one throwaway piece of practical information: Anthea made herself wake up at five in the morning by repeating to herself as she went to sleep, 'I must wake up at five o'clock' and banging her head five times on the pillow. I don't think I tried this out at the time, but the idea stuck with me and, when I was older, I practised setting an internal alarm clock. Eventually, I found that visualising setting an alarm in some 'other' part of my brain was surprisingly effective.

From that simple accomplishment, I learned that I could programme my 'back' brain to carry out more complex, useful functions like meeting deadlines of all kinds, finding solutions to intractable problems, germinating new ideas, and 'composting' books and other projects, without my conscious involvement. I realised I was doing this by actively accessing two seemingly separate states of my brain – Buddhism's intellect and intuition, Carl Jung's conscious and subconscious, Daniel Kahneman's thinking fast and slow, however you want to characterise them – and using them to do what each is best at. Without realising it, I developed a visualisation technique that only came to light when I was interviewed for a quirky radio programme in which the first question was 'What does the inside of your mind look like?'

Miss Moneypenny

Miss Moneypenny (wo)mans the front desk of your mind, is your day-to-day manager, critical thinker and conscious thought processes.

I realised that I have a very clear picture of the two functions of my mind: a 'front office' – my conscious mind – staffed by a brusque, efficient middle-aged woman (not me – a sort of Miss Moneypenny figure), working at a desk with computer screens, pads and pens, Post-It notes, pin boards and other office paraphernalia. She deals with incoming enquiries, does active planning and organising, logical analysis, keeps short term dates and times on the pin board and works office (waking) hours.

Behind her office chair is a door to the 'Library', which she never goes through herself, but she sends information, queries and requests through to the Librarian.

The Librarian

The Librarian works in mysterious ways in the subconscious recesses of your mind. She can access unknown information, send messages through dreams, gut feelings and creative thoughts.

The Library – my subconscious mind – is a dark Tardis-like space, the front of which is filled with rows and rows of old-fashioned green metal filing cabinets and shelving, but I can see, stretching into the distance, racks of computer servers and other increasingly hi-tech equipment. The Librarian wears a white lab coat and has the dishevelled air of an eccentric scientist. Her methods are obscure, but she works flexible hours, appears out of the gloom when needed, and always does the night shift.

Her access to weird and wonderful combinations of information means she is able to supply creative solutions, alarms and reminders, triggering unignorable gut responses and unexpected ideas (which must always be checked by the critical thinking of Miss Moneypenny). She also keeps track of a wider-ranging and longer-term schedule for me than Miss Moneypenny's daily pin board, and without my being aware of it, remembers birthdays and events, compiling virtual folders of the information I need to meet last-minute deadlines. On a just-in-time basis, she passes these through to Miss Moneypenny, who reminds me to act.

Miss Moneypenny can give the Librarian either specific or general instructions or requests for answers to difficult questions or solutions to challenging problems for particular dates or times – and she usually comes up with the goods, even if not necessarily in the way we expected. She's great on long-term projects like book 'composting', but it's important to trust her and not micro-manage her unfathomable processes, although she can be trained.

I have become aware that the Librarian and Miss Moneypenny can't work on the same assignment at the same time, so sometimes Miss M has to be distracted by mundane but demanding tasks like business admin, housework, accounts, dog walking or reading novels, to stop her interfering. I'm sure you'll have experienced a time when you were doing some basic or unrelated task and a genius idea popped into your head that you would never have come up with if you'd consciously tried to. That's what happens when you focus Miss Moneypenny's practical way of thinking on something other than the problem you want to solve, and leave the Librarian free access to find creative solutions.

My Miss Moneypenny was busy wrestling with Rethink Press profit and loss accounts when the Librarian suddenly, and unasked, presented the concept of this book, complete with title, in a neat package on her desk. Miss Moneypenny can have a tendency to work overtime, refusing to clock off when you're trying to relax or sleep. I find that listening to guided relaxation audios, or fiction audio books (set the Sleep Timer, or check the chapter number before you close your eyes) effectively ends her shift and allows the Librarian to start hers.

Returning to Keiron Sparrowhawk's five areas of cognition, Miss Moneypenny represents Attention, Working Memory and the conscious aspects of Executive Function; the Librarian covers Episodic Memory and more deeply embedded Executive

Function. The more closely they work in partnership, the better my Processing Speed.

My Librarian also represents a brain function called the Reticular Activating System – which is what gives you the ability to hear your own name spoken the other side of a packed room through the hubbub of a noisy party; to see every single silver Audi TT on the road when that's the car you've just set your heart on; and to hold a goal in mind and make it happen, even if not in the way you planned. When I was considering uprooting my London life to move to the country, a life coach suggested I draw a picture of the ideal house I wanted. I did, stuck it in a drawer and forgot about it, but the Librarian didn't. When I was packing to move to rural Norfolk, I found the drawing. The farmhouse we'd bought was almost identical, even in colour, to my drawing.

A few years later, I thought my career as a serial entrepreneur might need a safety net, so I took a teaching diploma in Adult Literacy and Creative Writing. It was brilliant up-skilling for business training, coaching, mentoring and presenting, but teaching practice made me realise I would never, ever be able to deal with the restrictions of the classroom environment, lesson plans, curricula and Ofsted inspections. Instead, I planned to start a business delivering writing training to the corporates I'd brought work-life balance to, and told people about my goal of teaching business people to write. But I never actively started to make this happen as I went back into publishing.

The Librarian, apparently, didn't give up on this goal, and delivered it precisely, but in an entirely different format than I had imagined. I became Publish Mentor to the Key Person of Influence programme, through which I 'train' hundreds of business people (entrepreneurs) every year to write their books.

In my experience, the female ability to multi-task (a contested description, but we know what it means) is at least partly based in having trained our minds, consciously or unconsciously, to operate resourcefully between the front office and library Executive Functions. Whether or not you use a visualisation technique like mine, you can make use of this ability to achieve your goal of writing and publishing your book, and to make the book-writing process timely and efficient by allowing your unique version of the Librarian to do background work 'while you're busy doing other things' (and The Angel has been locked in the attic), so it's ready and waiting for you, in neat folders on Miss Moneypenny's desk, when you sit down to write.

9

Mindset And Motivation

In the ABOO survey, I asked our circle of authors:

'How did you actually get your book written? How did you schedule writing time, working around other work and home commitments, keep up the momentum...?'

I also asked all the authors for their top five tips for those of you starting on your business or self-development book. The broad answers across these questions were remarkably consistent from all fifty of the ABOO Circle, with a fascinating variety of individual differences and quirks.

Tip #1 – believe in yourself

'Life for both sexes – and I looked at them, shouldering their way along the pavement – is arduous, difficult, a perpetual struggle. It calls for gigantic courage and strength. More than anything, perhaps, creatures of illusion as we are, it

calls for confidence in oneself. Without self-confidence we
are as babes in the cradle.'

Virginia Woolf, *A Room of One's Own*

The tip that was repeated more times than any other was around
mindset. The first essential step to take when writing a book of
one's own is to believe that you can do it; to have confidence in
your ability both to write a valuable book and to see the project
through.

'My vision outweighed the pain of the process.'

The words and phrases that came up repeatedly in comments
were:

Be brave!
Be bold!
Valuable
Non-negotiable
Expert
Success
mindset
Just
You can
do it!
Commit!
Original
Single-minded
Be selfish

'It's a struggle, that's for sure. But it seems to be a mindset game for me rather than a time-management issue.'

'We took a dose of our own medicine as we wrote in the first section of the book about the importance of a success mindset. Right at the start of the process we set the intention of achieving our goal. Working together was great. If one of us had a wobble, the other could provide coaching and support!'

From the long-term perspective of a writing mentor and a publisher, I can assure you that if you have at least three years' experience in your area of expertise, if you have a defined process that you take your clients through on a regular basis, if you are prepared to share your business and/or personal story, if you have case studies of clients that prove your process or system works, and if, as a bonus, you blog or write articles already, you certainly have the content for a good business book. If you also have an email list of 1,000+, and/or a following of 3,000+ across social media, and you or your business has a good and dependable income, you are in a strong position to invest in the production and promote your book.

'You **are** an expert in something; people do want to hear what you have to say.'

Beyond that, I can tell you with absolute confidence that if you follow the process of planning and writing your book that I'm going to share with you, you will produce a strong manuscript that will be ready for professional editing and publishing. If you believe that I know what I'm talking about, and what your fifty ABOO supporters are telling you, then you *can* have confidence in your own ability to plan and write a great book. And remember, this is not about writing a best seller and making a living from retail sales of your book; this is about writing a book that will speak to your market, your prospects, your clients and potential partners, and position you as an authority in your niche.

Members of the ABOO Circle said:

> 'Write for your tribe, not academic prowess.'

> 'Write it. As a business owner, your book is a key differentiator, so you've got to write it. I would say treat it as an asset, as a valuable investment. Make the time for it.'

Sandra Webber, coach and author of *Own It: regain control and live life on your terms*, advises you to reach out and set your own goals:

> 'Talk to somebody who's done it, somebody who has enjoyed doing it; people like that were the inspiration for me. The other thing is, ask yourself why are you doing it? Because when it gets difficult – and it will – or you're struggling, if you can go, "Right, this is why I'm doing it!" it will make all the difference. How I coach people is that if you can be comfortable being yourself and doing

something for your own reasons, you're not going to have to pretend to be something else, and then you're not going to get stressed. And it's the same with a book. You might have a fear that it has to be very polished, very spot-on. And I would say, no, it has to be real, it has to be you. The books that I relate to and the podcasts that I listen to are by people who can be genuine and authentic.'

Vicki Wusche, author of *The Wealthy Retirement Plan*, agrees that the route to confidence is to own your content:

'Women don't write books because they fear being criticised. But if it is your experience and your knowledge, how can I criticise it? I might have different knowledge and a different experience, but if you come from that place of "I'm just sharing what I know; this is my journey", you are less vulnerable. How can I knock you for your journey? It's your journey. Put in that mindset as a layer of protection.'

'One can only show how one came to hold whatever opinion one does hold.'
   Virginia Woolf, *A Room of One's Own*

Tip #2 – your book is your gift

The ABOO Circle wanted you to understand that maintaining your confidence, commitment and focus will depend on you being clear about who is going to benefit from you writing your book, and why you therefore have an obligation to get it done. In the short term, the ABOO authors are very aware, from their own experience, that while you are writing, some people may get less of your time and care; but in the long term, everyone will benefit. If, as women, we feel highly responsible for the wellbeing of others, both at work and at home, this is an attitude we can leverage to keep us on track with and committed to the book project.

Jane Frankland, author of *IN Security: Why a Failure to Attract and Retain Women in Cybersecurity is Making Us All Less Safe*, found a way to see that both her industry and her family would benefit from her book.

> 'The book came from a blog. I've been in the industry for over twenty years and I've built and sold my own global penetration testing (ethical hacking) company. I picked up a report by (ISC)2 and noticed that there were low numbers of women in the industry. Having been in it for so long, that really surprised me, but what actually bothered me more was seeing a trend. Numbers of women in the industry had dropped from about 18% in 2009 to 10% in 2015, and when I saw that, I just felt compelled

to write about it; I literally couldn't stop myself. I thought that I was going to get crucified for writing what I did, but I thought, "This is my view, it's my experience, no-one can take that away from me, and I need to be a voice," and so I did that.

I wrote the blog and I got really positive comments back from it, and after that I was asked to write more. Then I thought, "I'll turn it into a report, because that will add more value to the people out there," and it was at that point I told you I'd written this 15,000-word report.

I said, "Should I turn it into a book? It's got nothing to do with my business, but what should I do, Lucy?"

I think your exact words were, "You'd be crazy if you didn't do this." So that's how the book happened.

So, I think being clear on the value for readers can really help, but the other problem for women and writing books is that we usually have a ton of work to do. We might have family commitments or lots of other jobs around work that typically fall to us and we have the practicality of "What am I going to give up in order to do this?"

For me, writing the book was a sacrifice on family time. To begin with, I didn't actually realise how much time it was going to take, and I did pitch it to my children, why I was doing it, and they took that on board. It was hard on them, but when the box of books arrived, and my daughter held the physical book in her hand and read the acknowledgements at the beginning, she actually cried. That was really emotional because she knew what that had taken from all of us in terms of time investment. But both my sons and my daughter are so proud of the book, of being included in the book, so that's a really positive outcome.'

Sandra Webber, author of *Own It*, agrees that it can benefit the family:

'My two sons were quite surprised that I'd written a book. They're very proud of the fact. They're in their twenties, and my son talks about it at work, in his career, so he's getting a bit of kudos from it.'

Vicki Wusche looks at the value of her book to both her readers and her own business:

'When you're reaching the point where you think you want to write a book, because you've got some knowledge or some experience that you want to share, I would really think about "What's the purpose for me as an author and a businesswoman, and what is the purpose for you, the reader? What are you going to get out of it? How do I want you to think differently? What do I want you to do differently after reading my book? How will my book change you for the better, or make your life happier?"

And then also I need to make sure there is a business purpose to the book for me. Because they are costly, not just in terms of money, but in terms of the time that you take out of your business to write a book. So, I get very clear on those two things: who are you, the reader, and what do I want for you? And I need to know that there is something for me in this process.'

The tips from many of us include to continually keep in mind, at the start and throughout your book project, who your book will help. Write a list of the key beneficiaries and stick it somewhere it's constantly in view – near where you work, on your laptop or on your fridge. Focus especially on what your book will be gifting to your readers, the knowledge and experience you will be passing on to so many more people than you can ever meet in person. Think constantly about what you know that will help them to understand themselves or others better, to run more efficient businesses, make more money, lead happier lives, or be inspired to take action.

One member of the ABOO Circle had a straightforward and poignant motivation:

'I wanted my dad to see I'd published a book. And feeling I had something new to say that was important enough to share, and **should** be shared for everyone's wellbeing and business productivity.'

10

You're Not Alone

The ABOO Circle want you to appreciate the importance of support from, and accountability to, other key people during your writing process.

Tip #3 – it's a team effort

On the professional side, most agreed that working with a mentor, coach, accountability group or partner, or having a publisher on board from the start, was key to them successfully negotiating and completing the journey.

On the personal front, getting support and buy-in from a partner, your family, close friends and relatives, and work colleagues is also an essential lifeline for getting through. Even telling clients and announcing their book to the wider market on their websites, blogs or social media helped many of the ABOO authors stay the course.

They talked about:

Support network **Accountability** **Cheerleaders** group **Coach** Your tribe **Friends** **Publisher** Accountability **Family** Your Crowd buddy **Editor** **Colleagues**

'I got myself a book coach – who said I could write a book in ninety days, so I followed her process. She coached me and set me targets every week and I actually found the process relatively easy once I got started. About halfway through, my mum was taken very ill, but somehow I kept going – I was motivated for her to see the finished book.'

'I used a mentor to keep me accountable and her team to do all publishing (I just wrote).'

It's worth repeating that to make your book valuable to you, your business, your market and your readers, you have to write the best book you can. Certainly, one way to ensure your book presents you to your market and the world in the best and most professional way is to work with a book mentor.

These are my top tips for getting the best out of a mentor:

Research what book mentors do – there are also writing coaches, ghost-writers and structural editors who offer different but sometimes overlapping services. When you are clear what a mentor offers and that this is what you are looking for…

Look online and talk to other authors about mentors they have worked with, and how. Get some recommendations and check out the ones you like the sound of. Talk to each of them and ask questions about the way they would work with you, how they can deliver the outcomes you expect, and raise any concerns you have – nothing is too unimportant to get clear about. Expect them to be open about what they can't deliver, as well as what they can. Fees vary; to a large extent, you pay for experience and outcomes.

Choose a mentor who understands your goals for writing and publishing your book. They don't have to be an expert in your field, but they should understand who your market is and how you want to position yourself in it. You should be confident that they have experience in the current publishing environment and will give you honest, unbiased advice. Work with a mentor you like, respect and trust.

Making the writing process manageable. One of your mentor's jobs is to make the task of planning and writing your book manageable. They should reduce the overwhelm by breaking the process down into discrete steps that need to be taken one at a time and in the right order. An experienced book mentor will have a tried and tested process they take their authors through that they can clearly outline to you up front, demonstrating how it has worked for others.

Use your mentor for accountability. Many aspiring authors set themselves goals and timetables that too easily get put aside when life or work gets demanding. Work with your mentor to reverse engineer a schedule, the endpoint of which is either your final manuscript or the published book. Be realistic about the time you can give to writing, and take note of your mentor's experience of what is achievable. Agree waypoints that they will hold you accountable to.

Positioning, planning and structuring. Your mentor will help you create a compelling working title that will attract your market and potential publishers. They will ensure you have a detailed structure for your book in place before you start any writing. If you've developed this yourself, let them review it and interrogate you about any potential weak points, lack of logic or detail. If they are helping you create the book blueprint, take the time to get it right so you're both happy with the reader journey before you start writing.

Lean on your mentor early on. The first ten thousand words you write will be the hardest. This is the time when you most need your mentor to check in on your writing, give clear and detailed feedback, and be there to reassure you when you (inevitably) have misgivings about the whole project. Once you've got into the writing habit, found your author voice and started ticking off items on your contents list, you will feel more confident and need less input.

A steady hand. Writing is an emotional business and a piece of valuable self-development. As you get your first draft written, you'll go through ups and downs, crises of confidence, flashes of genius, worries that your book is too long, too short – all typical writing stages that your mentor will recognise and offer objectivity that you will sometimes lack. Keep in regular contact with your mentor, share your feelings as well as your progress.

Sometimes writing your business book will give you insights into your practices and processes that lead to changes both in the business and to the book. An experienced business book mentor will understand and help you manage such outcomes, and refer you to other specialist business mentors if necessary.

Overview and detailed feedback. Your mentor is not an editor, but they should review your first draft and give you an overview of your manuscript and specific pointers for the next step – your first self-edit. They can help you identify beta readers for the second draft of your manuscript and ensure you get the most useful feedback. You may get contested and contradictory responses from your readers, and your mentor is the ideal person to help you sift and incorporate this feedback.

Publication and promotion. Your book mentor should be well placed to advise you on the best route to publication for you and your book. They will be able to explain the pros and cons of traditional publishing, DIY self-publishing or hybrid publishing. An experienced mentor will have contacts in all areas of publishing and be able to review offers, options and contracts with you. They can continue to work with you as the book comes out and advise you on how to achieve the goals that you started this process with.

For some of you, the support of a professional coach or mentor will be less important than the synergy and even competition of a group or a buddy engaged in the same book-writing process as you.

Tara Halliday, author of *Unmasking: The Coach's Guide to Impostor Syndrome*, described how she worked with her accountability buddy.

'It was absolutely essential for me to have an accountability buddy and to work with somebody who had the same level of motivation as me. We both wanted to write our books pretty quickly: it took us six weeks to write our first draft and we would call each other once a week. There would be no excuses and we'd set ourselves a word count.

I had someone to answer to, which was the most helpful thing. It's just so much harder to try and do it by yourself, particularly if as a woman you have the idea that it's a little bit selfish or there are other better things that you should be doing.

One of the reasons I was interested in having my accountability buddy, who was a man, was that he was competitive, and his competitiveness brought out and helped along my competitiveness as well. It made it fun, but it did add that element. If I'd had maybe a more laidback man or woman, rather than somebody who's quite competitive and keen to get something done really quickly, I think we might've drifted a bit.

When we started, our very first week, he'd been busy so I'd written more words than him. And he hated that, but it spurred him on. This is what I mean about the competitiveness. And because he was spurred on, he gave himself a higher word count, so I said, "I'm going to write 5,000 words this week." And he'd say, "I'm going to write 6,000 words."

This is a mass generalisation, but women might tend to be more supportive and understanding, so they might need to take their responsibility as accountability buddy more seriously. We're not there to support each other in terms of this. We're there to get this job done. No excuses. That's how we got our first draft written in six weeks.'

So be careful about being a Big Sister to your accountability group or buddy. This is about *you* getting *your* book written.

However, numerous studies[37] have shown that women prefer working co-operatively in groups while men prefer working alone. One of the reasons for this is that women have a higher opinion of their colleagues' or co-workers' abilities and less confidence in their own, while men have a (not necessarily justified) higher opinion of their own abilities than they do in anyone else's. Women also tend to prefer egalitarian working structures and outcomes, whereas men favour competitive and hierarchical

37 https://www.theatlantic.com/business/archive/2013/08/why-women-prefer-working-together-and-why-men-prefer-working-alone/278888/

structures.[38] Small groups of women writing their books together ('microenvironments'[39]) may be a particularly effective way for us to increase the number of female-authored business books.

Whether you work with a professional coach or mentor, involve your publisher or editor during the writing process, surround yourself with a group of like-minded authors, or compete with an accountability buddy, you need people on your team to help you through the writing process. The first draft is the hardest and when you need to draw most on support. But it's also important that the people closest to you, at work or at home, understand why you are investing your time and energy (and possibly money) in the book, and act as your back-up team. Their input on this level is another emotional stake you can use to leverage up your commitment: if your book is reducing your time with your family and/or business, all the more reason for you to commit to getting it done as fast and efficiently as possible.

ABOO Circle members said:

> 'I started telling my friends and family, so they would keep me accountable. In the end I had to cut back on work, knuckle down and do it.'

---

38 https://www.sheknows.com/living/articles/5740/women-work-better-in-teams/

39 https://phys.org/news/2015-04-women-benefit-woman-dominated-teams.html

'I redirected time from sales and marketing to writing. Consequently, my business took quite a hit in the time I was writing the book. I used my daily runs as thinking time, time on trains as writing time, time at weekends as research time, and time out walking with my husband as mentoring time.'

'Your family will survive without you!'

11

Preparation Is Everything

I decided that for my third book, a novel about families, parents, children born and adopted, I was going to do my own thing, get in the flow, be totally creative and original, and not be constrained by anyone or anything else. I started writing what was mainly a thinly disguised tale of part of my own life, and over a couple of months I wrote regularly, got thoroughly into the creative process, felt stimulated, imaginative and in the flow, sure I was producing a unique and ground-breaking piece of work.

I finished a first draft, printed it out and sent it to a literary agent I knew. A fortnight later I had a letter back from her: she told me my manuscript was both boring and unbelievable.

I rang her up, sure she must have made a mistake, that I could convince her to re-assess my work.

'It can't be unbelievable,' I whined. 'It's true – that's my life.'

'Truth and fiction are not the same thing,' she snapped. 'There's no structure to your story and that makes it unreadable.'

The penny dropped. I realised that because I'd given myself over to the writing process, felt creative and written from a sense of being in flow, I'd missed out the most basic and important step in writing anything, but especially something as long as a book: planning and structure.

I processed her response, got over myself, and spent some time researching story structure, from theories like *The Hero's Journey*, to the neuroscience of storytelling, to straightforward tips on organising plots, subplots, themes and characters. Later I wrote my own book on the subject, *How To Write Fiction Without The Fuss*. And don't think this isn't relevant to business writing too.

I took the bones of my first story and turned it into a proper novel concept. I wrote a 'bible' of the characters and their development, settings, background, and a summary of the plot; then I created a detailed chapter outline, where I could see the rise and fall, and interweaving of the main plot and subplots as they unfolded on the page. I wrote three chapters in which I could feel the main character's voice developing and a sense of tension building... and then I stuffed them into a drawer and forgot about them.

In 2004, Richard and Judy launched their Book Club, and opened it with a competition for a new and original novel; the winner would be published by Macmillan. I saw the ads and decided not to enter – but the few friends who had read my second version chapters urged me to give it a go. On the day before the deadline,

I revised and printed out the synopsis, re-typed my three chapters into one and submitted them.

Six months later, I got a letter from Macmillan saying that though my entry hadn't won, of the 47,000 entries they'd received, mine was one of another ten they'd like to publish. Could they see the rest of the manuscript? Of course, there was no 'rest', but they gave me three months to complete it, and I did.

This time I was not going to leave anything to chance, so I worked with a writing coach to keep me on track, and my friend and editor, Verity Ridgman (now Senior Editor at Rethink Press), read the book in chunks as I wrote it. And finally, my reading group read the whole manuscript and gave me useful feedback.

Blood and Water was published a year later, followed by two more novels.

My point here is that detailed structure and planning, before you start writing, is key to the success of any book. And every book, fictional or otherwise, takes the reader on a journey – a story of sorts – that they will find easy or hard, engaging or tedious, memorable or forgettable, convincing or not – that is based on its structure.

Brian Tracy, author of *No Excuses: the Power of Self-Discipline* and *Eat That Frog* – all useful messages in terms of book writing – says:

'Every minute you spend in planning saves 10 minutes in execution; this gives you a 1,000 percent return on energy!'

Tip #4 – plan and position

The ABOO Circle also made planning one of their top tips. Spending time planning the structure of your book in detail is absolutely essential to writing efficiently, without experiencing writer's block or going off track and having to rewrite. So, if you're going to do the best for yourself, your readers, and your supporters at home and at work who are taking the hit from your writing schedule, invest in planning time.

The ABOO Circle used the following words repeatedly in their comments on this question:

In describing their book creation process, almost everyone said they had started with a detailed plan – many of them worked with a professional on this stage in particular, even if not through the whole writing process.

Audrey Chapman, author of *Love Selling*, described her journey:

'Once I'd made the decision to write my book, I mulled it around in my head for three to four months. I spent a further month gathering any previous work I'd done that could be useful. I did a little research to check I hadn't missed anything out, then had a number of sessions with my coach to talk through and sense-check my thought process.

I trust him implicitly, so this was an extremely useful time for me – getting away from others who thought I was crazy or deluded was imperative. Negative influences who thought they were offering "sensible" advice would have made it even more difficult to manage the process. It's hard putting yourself out there. It's also hard being positive when you have naysayers around you.

I booked a BookPlan session with Rethink Press to help me refine my thinking and then I went away for six weeks, on my own, to write my book. I had specifically cleared my diary of work and home commitments for this time, and I'm pretty good with deadlines, so I knew that I would do whatever it took to complete the first draft.'

Notice that Audrey's process of decision-making, mulling, re-searching, discussing and planning, while she was continuing with life and work as normal, took around six months. And it was this combination of first letting her Librarian mind work intuitively followed by structured Moneypenny planning that allowed her to take a comparatively short scheduled time out to complete her first draft in six weeks.

I use a model called *P-L-A-N* to help authors position both themselves and their book for their market. It stands for *P*osition, *L*isten, *A*mbition, *N*iche Vision.

There are two aspects to the first step – *Position*: how you want to position yourself as the author of this book; and positioning the book so it appeals to your ideal client, the recipient of the book as 'business card'.

To clarify your own position of authority, you might want to make some brief notes on: your position in your industry; your unique experience – including any failures as well as successes; external validation of your expertise, such as credentials or qualifications; the difference between you and your competitors. Name some individuals or businesses that you have helped – name-drop, if possible; and summarise the outcomes you achieved for these clients.

'So long as you write what you wish to write, that is all that matters; and whether it matters for ages or only for hours, nobody can say.'
Virginia Woolf, *A Room of One's Own*

Your notes will help you to position yourself and to write, as you will need to at some point, a 250-word author bio to go inside your book, and a three-sentence version for the back cover.

Next, it's important to clarify exactly who you are writing your book for. Some authors with a broad subject matter can be tempted to say their book is for 'anyone and everyone'. Even a traditional publisher, looking for maximum retail sales, won't be happy with that answer – every book has to be sold from a section or shelf in a bookshop, or a handful of categories on Amazon. But for a business book author, who has other reasons for publishing than to achieve retail sales, it is better to focus right down on one or two ideal clients as the reader you are writing for.

To position your book to your market, consider: your ideal client's business or type of business; their position in your/their industry; your ideal client's turnover or income (an amount below which they're unlikely to be able to afford your services); and what their three top motivations for using your services would be. Try to define your ideal client's age range/gender/circumstances, and then give a name to a current, past or future ideal client.

From this information, it can be very helpful to create an avatar of Your Ideal Client – the individual or decision-maker in a business you would most love to work with. They may be a theoretical concept at this point, or they could be someone you know but haven't made contact with yet, or someone who has already been your client and you'd like to attract more like them. Write a description, draw a picture, find an actual photo – and write your book as a one-to-one conversation with that person. It will also help you find your author voice when you start writing.

Niching your book to a single person won't restrict your audience – it will just direct your valuable information to the people most valuable to you.

'Write the book for one person only.'

Now you know who your book is aimed at, you can *Listen* to your ideal client to find out what they want to hear from you. Ask yourself, what are your ideal client's biggest problems and what issues are they facing in their business or work; how do these impact on them personally; and what will happen if their problem persists? Write down the three top questions your prospects and clients regularly ask you, and the key solutions you always provide for your clients.

Knowing and appealing to your ideal clients' underlying problems tells you the position they will be in when they're going to come looking for help through your book; the point in their business or personal journey at which you need to meet them with your solution.

And then you can ask yourself, what is your *Ambition* for your reader when they've read your book? What is the underlying solution that all your ideal clients will want you to provide? To do that, you need to unpack exactly how you improve their business, work or life. What is the unique solution that you offer your clients; how does it differ from other solutions or challenge conventional wisdom in your area? List the benefits your readers or ideal clients will get if they take your advice or implement your solution.

And finally, the content of your book will be based on the *Niche Vision* that is your service or product. What is the process you take all your clients through? Writing it out for your book is a great chance to standardise and develop it into defined steps, and perhaps create a model, such as an acronym like *P-L-A-N* or the *WRITER Process*, a metaphor like a toolbox or climbing a mountain, a graphic like the Urgent/Important matrix or Bloom's Taxonomy, or a number of steps like The Twelve Step Programme. If your process is not unique in itself, you must apply it in a unique method.

Within an overarching process, you may have tools, tips or techniques that are your own creations. It is helpful to reference some research, data or other objective information that supports your way of working and can be cited in your book. And vital to a good business book, which is not salesy but sells you and your services under the radar, are case studies and examples, preferably from your own clients, to illustrate your theories and 'hard' content.

Compost

Once you have made notes on the four aspects of *P-L-A-N,* I advise you to take a few days, weeks, or even – like Audrey – months to let these concepts process. Having stimulated your book mindset, you will find yourself in a heightened state of awareness and new ideas will float up from the library of your subconscious, while books you read, things people say, the media, social and otherwise, will seem to crackle with relevant information. This internal development is the first step to creating a strong piece of writing and is not one that should be skipped.

After the process of immersing yourself in your clients'/readers' questions and problems and the answers and solutions you can offer in your book – sometimes evocatively referred to as 'composting', and only you can know when you've done enough composting – it's time to take the first step in externalising your work.

Plan

'Planning and strategy: we spent time right at the start
of the process planning the content. We got creative with
coloured pens, mind-maps, Post-It notes and flip-charts.
This plays to our style; others may prefer to use lists,
spreadsheets, mood-boards or Pinterest. Once we had the
high-level topics, we broke them down into bullet points
and developed a strategy for writing the content in each
area of the table of contents. At any given point we were
writing a paragraph, rather than having the daunting task
of writing a book. This made it easier to keep track of
where we were and milestones as we progressed. We were
clear of the timeline, we were committed to achieving
each milestone, and we made ourselves accountable to our
publisher to ensure we hit the deadlines.'

Lyn Bromley and Donna Whitbrook, authors
*Trusted: the human approach to building outstanding
client relationships in a digitised world*

Lyn and Donna suggest starting the planning process with
'high-level topics', such as big sections and chapter headings. This
can work well if you already have a clear grasp of the detailed
content of your book. I prefer to work with authors from the
bottom up, getting them to list as many topics as they can think
of on index cards, topics that could cover between 500 and 1,000
words – think blog-post or article – as a first step. Assembling
between thirty and forty of these gives you the content for a

whole book, which often pleasantly surprises authors. Your cards can then be shuffled into related areas that become your chapters and, if appropriate, grouped into bigger sections or parts – think beginning, middle and end.

> 'I worked with a Rethink book coach, and we started off by looking at what the topics were, then what the chapters were going to be, and then how it was going to be structured. She helped me with that and really gave me the confidence to write. And one of the things that really helped me was actually approaching each chapter as a blog, because when I first knew that I was going to write the book, it was quite overwhelming. I thought, "How am I going to do this?" So, simply by changing the way that I viewed it, I knew that I could write blog posts, so I adopted that mentality.'
>
> **Jane Frankland, author *IN Security***

Everyone has a different preferred style. At one end of the spectrum, mind maps with lots of colour, maybe drawings and icons, are an excellent starting point for the very visual; cards and Post-It notes give a kinaesthetic and flexible feel to your book content; while word- and list-orientated people like me prefer to go straight for a typed up list of contents.

The fact is, a book is a word-by-word, line-by-line, left-to-right, top-to-bottom, page-by-page narrative medium, and however you structure the planning process, a highly detailed written-out contents list is the best blueprint to work from when you start writing.

> 'Definitely plan. Just plan the life out of it, and then writing becomes so much easier. Get a big sheet of blank paper. Write something in the middle, a theme, a sentence that appeals, and then let your thoughts go. Just get every thought that's in your head about the topic, and if you can do mind mapping, do mind mapping. If Post-It notes work better for you… but just get all of the thoughts out of your head.
>
> And once you've got those thoughts out of your head and onto paper, then the book actually almost writes itself. And the only other tip is, write about something that you're passionate about. That also makes it much easier to write. If you are passionate about it, and you really have a message that you want to get out there, then again the words will just flow.'
>
> **Marianne Page, author *Simple, Logical, Repeatable***

Structure

Here's a basic book structure that the majority of business books will fit into:

Front Matter – 1,000 words

Praise quotes (approximately six short paragraphs over two pages)*

Copyright/imprint page

Contents Page

Dedication (short)*

Foreword (500 words, written by someone else)*

*Optional

Introduction – 1,500 words

Who you are (brief version of your personal/ business story)

Why you're writing the book

Who it's for

What their problem is

How you will solve it in the book

Part One* (eg, Beginning, Status Quo or Theory)

Includes 2–5 CHAPTERS – Up to 10,000 words

Each chapter contains 3 to 5 topics, illustrated consistently with case studies, top tips, research, etc.

Part Two* (eg, Middle, Main Content or Model)

Includes 2–5 CHAPTERS – Up to 10,000 words

Each chapter contains 3 to 5 topics, illustrated consistently with case studies, top tips, research, etc.

Part Three* (eg, End, Implementation or Outcomes)

Includes 2–5 CHAPTERS – Up to 10,000 words

Each chapter contains 3 to 5 topics, illustrated consistently with case studies, top tips, research, etc.

Conclusion/Summary 500–1,000 words

Main points of your book

What the reader now knows

What the future holds for them

What they should do next (contact you, further free info…)

Back Matter – 1,000 words

References/Further Reading*

Acknowledgements: thank anyone and everyone

The Author (300-word bio ending in your website and social media contact details + B&W hi-res headshot)

*Optional

Total Word Count: *typically, 34,000*

'A clear vision, backed by definite plans, gives you a tremendous feeling of confidence and personal power.'
Brian Tracy, *Great Little Book on the Gift of Self-confidence*

12

Start Writing

Of all the tips and techniques offered by the ABOO contributors, they were most forthcoming about the ways in which they had managed to actually get their books written. Every single one of our fifty women authors had created a slightly different schedule, worked around their family and business in individual ways, discovered their optimum writing times and taken varying lengths of time to complete their book.

Tip #5 – prioritise and write

Through the surveys and interviews came a huge sense of pride in the ABOO Circle's achievements and a real desire to encourage and inspire you to get your book written and published.

The same words were repeated many times:

'I was *really* disciplined! I couldn't cut down on client work as I have a mortgage to pay, so weekends became writing time. I did the 10-day challenge with Alison Jones which convinced me I could make time. After that I created a chapter-by-chapter plan from where I was, through editing, proofs and to publication. I didn't let myself slip more than one task before pulling it back. Looking back, I'm astounded how I did it!'

'Balls of steel. I calculated I needed x words per week, therefore x words per day. I set a deadline. I told everybody about the deadline. I made it happen.'

From mentoring business book authors over the years, and reviewing what has worked for the majority of writers, I've developed a model called *The WRITER Process* which chunks down your book-writing process into six discrete steps – *Write* (your first draft), *Review* and *Improve* (your first self-edit), *Test* (your second draft with beta readers), *Edit* (incorporate feedback), and *Repeat* (as required).

Step 1 – Write

This step has three key elements which you need to establish in order.

1. Make sure you have planned the structure and content of your book in detail. List your chapter headings, three or four sub-sections in each and any additional material you will include, such as case studies, quotes or illustrations. Plan for an introductory paragraph for each chapter where you tell the reader what you're going to tell them, and a summary where you tell them what you've told them. A consistent format for each chapter makes your content easier for you to write and your reader to absorb.

> 'I started by writing a detailed structure for my book. I set myself a target of 500 words per morning a couple of times a week before doing anything else. Sometimes I wrote a lot more and other times, not so much. My only rule was that I had to sit for an hour and write. The days I felt uninspired ended up being dedicated to research on the topic, which inevitably fired me up by reminding me of just how much there was to say!'

2. How long is your book going to be? It might sound like 'how long is a piece of string?', but this is something you should decide in advance. A good average word length for a business or self-development book is 30,000 to 40,000 words, in which you can get across substantial information, but it can be read and absorbed quickly by your reader. More than 50,000 words begins to feel like hard work (for you and the reader); fewer than 20,000 words makes for a slim volume.

Divide your chosen word count by the number of chapters you have in your contents list – leaving 1,500 for an Introduction and 1,000 for a Summary chapter. Then decide how many words you will write per week and when. A majority of ABOO authors found early morning – very early morning in some cases – the best time for them.

> 'Get up early – two hours early, write for an hour every day, then go back to bed for an hour.'

> 'I would get up at six in the morning and write for six days per week before my actual day would start. I committed to 1,000 to 2,000 words on those days.'

> 'I set my alarm for 4.30am. Got up, wrote in peace for two hours before going back to bed, to be woken with tea and toast at 8.30am.'

It may be hard at first, but stick to your scheduled writing times, making them as regular and similar as possible (same place, same time, same props, such as the same mug of tea or coffee, same tracks if you write to music). Your writer's mind will soon see these as triggers to work, and switch into creative mode on cue. Schedule writing time into your diary or planner with high importance status. If you miss an appointment with your book, make it up asap.

3. Make it your goal to get your first full draft written as quickly as possible. If there are areas where you find you lack content, research or case studies, don't stop. Make a note, leave a space and move on.

ABOO authors said:

> 'For my first book, I wrote longhand in a café during my lunchbreaks at work and then typed it up at the weekends. For my first book I was motivated to get it produced before my 30th birthday. For subsequent books, editors gave me a deadline.'

> 'Don't worry about your spelling, grammar or punctuation, whether you've perfectly expressed your ideas or been as witty as you'd hoped. Leave a star or note in the margin where you know more work is required later.'

> 'Write it quickly – go for it with gusto!'

> 'Don't worry if it's not perfect, you can always improve it with further versions.'

You don't have to write your first draft in chronological order. If you get stuck in a chapter, move on to another one that inspires you more and come back to the original one later. Keep your contents list to hand and tick off the completed sections till they're all written.

Lisette Schuitemaker has written four books, including *The Eldest Daughter Effect* and *Childless Living*, and has honed her process and her understanding of what it takes to write a book.

'The only way that I can do it is if I block it in my diary and I take that appointment as seriously as any other appointment. So, I usually block say from 8.30am to 12.30pm and say I don't do meetings in the mornings and I take no calls in the mornings. Of course, I make exceptions, but really the only way to write is to write. And to make the time for it.

When an idea for a book comes to me, I think about it for a while, to see if I'm willing to spend a year or two years with this topic, because there's research, then there's the writing, then there's the whole process of editing and proof reading and all that. And then, of course, there's the talking about it. It is a bit… it's not a child, I will not say that. I'm not a mother. But it is a thing that you live with for a while and I think women in business know this, once you've committed to a new product or a new venture or a new service, you go with it. You have to fall in love with it.'

Steps 2 and 3 – Review and Improve

First, and genuinely important, is to take a break at the end of your first draft. Give yourself a few days at the very least, maybe a week, without giving your first draft a glance. It might be that you need longer than a week to put space between yourself and your manuscript – let your intuition, rather than your enthusiasm to get published, guide you on this.

> 'Once you think the book is complete, have a break from it for a few weeks and then read it through with new eyes.'

When you return to your book, if you haven't already, make a note of your total word count, and the word count of each chapter. Also make sure you have formatted your manuscript in 12pt Arial or Times New Roman (the easiest fonts to read that everyone will have) with 1.5 line spacing and at least an inch of margin all round.

Now print out your entire manuscript. A crucial aspect of reviewing your work is to step outside your writer mode and into reader mode; reading your own words on paper gives you more separation than if you return to them on the screen. You need as much objectivity and distance as possible to identify where there are gaps, repetitions, inconsistencies or actual errors. Work through your whole book, slowly and carefully, always with a pen in hand, making copious notes.

This step is not proofreading or editing; it's not about correcting spelling errors or your grammar (just mark them if you come across any obvious mistakes); it is about assessing whether the structure of your book works; whether your 'story' leads the reader through the information in a logical and compelling way. As you read, make constant notes on your manuscript about your own responses. If your total word count is greater than you planned or wanted, mark up where you can trim or cut elements. If any one of your chapters is markedly longer or shorter than the others, look especially hard for ways to reduce or increase its content.

When you've worked through to the end, switch back into writer mode and return to your electronic manuscript with your paper notes by your side to *Improve*.

If you have found issues with the content itself, deal with this first, particularly if it means an overhaul of the objective or message of the book is in order. Don't be disheartened by the prospect of substantial reworking; even if you need to take some processing time before getting down to it, the solution will present itself and your book will be the better for dealing with it at this stage rather than later in the process.

Structural problems need to be looked at next: you might have decided that a complete chapter is in the wrong place and needs moving, or sections within one or more of the chapters should be re-ordered. Remember when you do this to check all other references to this aspect of the book, and look at the chapter or section holistically again when you have finished.

After that, sorting out the lesser concerns of filling gaps in content, adding case studies, carrying out additional research, trimming material or sharpening up the presentation of your ideas will clarify the content in your own mind as well as in those of your readers.

When you've done your best to fix your big picture issues, work through the manuscript from start to finish, correcting every point you've noted from your review, and anything else that shows up as you progress.

Keep an eye out for consistency as you improve the second draft of your book. Ensure that your chapters are all a similar (not necessarily identical) length; that the sections within each chapter are similarly divided up; and that chapters are all structured in the same way. Each chapter must start with some kind of introduction, and end with a summary.

Step 4 – Test

You've written a first draft, stood back from your manuscript to review it, and then improved your book as much as you can for the moment. Now the most important thing you can do is ask a few trusted colleagues to give you their honest opinion.

'Get frequent feedback. Hearing other people's opinion about something you poured your heart and soul into is a bit vulnerable and painful at first – but it gets easier with time.'

Your choice of beta reader is important and will affect the quality of the feedback you receive. Ideal candidates are:

- Two or three colleagues, who know your subject matter to at least the same depth as you and can tell you how well you have covered the material, where you have gaps to fill or made any factual errors.

- Trusted clients or customers (two or three, max) who represent your target market will give you valuable insight into how well you've engaged your readers and offered them practical solutions to the problems they experience in your niche area.

- A key person in your industry who you feel comfortable approaching to ask this favour of. People are usually flattered to be asked their opinion of a book manuscript, and this person may be someone who could write you a Foreword – or at least a praise quote – if they like what they read and feel invested enough to promote your book in your market.

- Another author or editor who specialises in your genre of book. This could be the professional editor you're going to work with: if you ask them to get involved at this stage, they could carry out a 'structural edit' and give you detailed feedback on your structure, content and writing style, but you would need to pay them for this piece of work in addition to the copy edit your final manuscript will need as part of your publishing process.

Family and friends are not ideal beta readers, for obvious reasons.

Be clear with your *Test* readers about what sort of feedback you want from them: it must be honest, specific and constructive, including positive reactions as well as improvements they think you could make. Request politely that they get the job done by an agreed deadline. Make sure they know you do not want them to edit your manuscript, and to ignore spelling and grammar issues.

Step 5 – Edit

When you get the feedback from your beta readers, enjoy the positives, but accept any honest negative responses at this stage as a gift. They may save you from rejection by agents or publishers, or bad reviews from critics or paying readers.

First collate all your feedback. It might not all be consistent; your readers may disagree with each other and take different points of view. Take seriously anything that two or more readers do agree on. Try to assess criticism objectively, even though you'd rather listen to the praise. Decide which suggestions you are going to accept and implement – in the end, this is your book.

Once you have finessed your book in terms of the wider issues, it's time to edit the manuscript for fine detail. If you have made any major revisions and done any extensive rewriting, it could be helpful to take another break before you start the close work on syntax and style.

In addition to checking your style, paragraph and sentence construction, make sure you:

- Check your facts – dates, science, events, numbers, people's names, accurate quotations…

- Vary your vocabulary and sentence structure – try not to use the same word more than once in a paragraph; find different ways to express yourself.

- Read aloud for rhythm – if any sentence doesn't feel quite right, read it aloud to discover where it's losing pace or tying itself in knots.

- Get up to speed with grammar – if you're not already a grammar nerd, buy a handbook on grammar and punctuation and look up anything you're not sure of. Clarity of expression leads to clarity of thought.

Step 6 – Repeat

Repeat the last two steps as many times as will bring your book closest to perfection. But perfection is not required from you – that's the job of a professional editor, ideally provided by your publisher.

13

Getting Your Book Out There

'The hard bit comes later – I had a pre-publishing meltdown and lost all confidence. It's sometimes not the bits you think will be hard that are!'

Tip #6 – publish and promote

There are three main routes to getting your book published:

1. Traditional Publishing – in this business model, the publisher takes financial responsibility for preparation, production and publication of a book, and makes a return on their investment from book sales. You may lose copyright, control, and royalties will not be high. Traditional publishers will be looking for their return on investment from retail sales.

Traditional publishing can be ideal if you:

* Are already a high-profile expert in your area

* Have a broad niche book

- Can prove a 5,000+ following, client base, email list that you regularly interact with

- Have a credible personal marketing strategy for promoting your book

- Are not in a hurry to publish – it is likely to take a year from signature of contract

2. (Do It Your) Self-Publishing – as the author, you invest your time and money in preparing and publishing your own book, then make 100% of the money from book sales and/or leveraging your book for increased income from your work or business. 'Self-publishing' is a misnomer, as it is impossible to publish a high-quality book without sourcing, paying and project-managing professionals such as editors, cover designers, typesetters, e-book converters, and learning publishing technology.

DIY self-publishing can be ideal if you:

- Are on a tight budget

- Have professional design skills

- Enjoy project management, learning new skills and have time to spare from your own business

- Intend to publish many books

- See your books as products and plan to recoup your investment through retail sales, like a fiction author

'I would go so far then as to say that if somebody's self-publishing, you're better off not doing it unless you're going to make it look like it hasn't been self-published, which is not easy to do.'

3. Hybrid (paid for) Publishing – you, the author, pay a professional publisher to prepare, produce and publish your book (the same function as a traditional publisher, but with a different business model), then make a return on investment through leveraging your book for impact, income and influence, and in some cases book sales too. The publisher doesn't require you to sell loads of retail copies.

Hybrid publishing can be ideal if you:

- Have a successful, established business with existing products or services

- Have a marketing budget to pay professionals

- Want to maintain control over your book content and design

- Are used to excellent service and quality results

- Understand that giving away books will give a better return on investment (ROI) than book sales

There can be confusion between self-publishing and hybrid publishing caused by some, sometimes unscrupulous, paid-for publishing services companies calling themselves 'self-publishing' companies. This also is a misnomer. A self-publisher (or indie publisher) is an author who has taken the time and trouble to project manage all aspects of the publication process (often outsourcing key tasks) and has purchased their own ISBNs – effectively becoming an independent micro-publisher in their own right.

It's a good idea to consider your publishing options early on in your writing process, so you can either write a proposal for a traditional publisher, sign up with a hybrid publisher, or start looking for the freelance professionals you will need to co-ordinate to work on your self-published book. You'll also know in good time how long the publishing process is going to take, when you can call on support from your team, and whether you are working to a deadline.

Your ABOO Circle had their books published in a variety of ways, with the majority having chosen hybrid publishing.

Once the writing is over and the publishing process is underway – although there's still plenty of work for you to do during this phase – it's time to think about how you're going to promote your book once it's published. It seems that as women, we are not all the best at self-promotion or marketing, which undermines our authority and the other benefits we should be enjoying from sharing our experience and making a difference in the world. It is not easy, as Audrey Chapman told me, but it is worth it:

'I'm coming up to the second anniversary of my book being published. The first twelve months were exceptionally hard work, looking for opportunity everywhere and anywhere: looking for opportunities to speak publicly (I've spoken at a London event of 250 people through to a Llama Park in Sussex with five women!); hustling to engage with the kind of clients I desired to work with; trying, successfully and unsuccessfully, new marketing strategies; and generally doing whatever I could to get things off the ground.

Being in start-up phase is not for the faint-hearted. But in year two, everything started to fall into place. My income has now reached a level that I'm pleased with.'

We know from research in a range of fields that while men will ask for what they consider is their due – whether it's promotion, pay rises, respect or position – women tend to wait quietly for their contribution to be acknowledged and praised. While this can work, it's not enough to get your book out into the world and bringing value to you and your business, your readers and your market. Once again, we have to tap into our tendency to prioritise other people's needs before our own and use it to get our book read by as many people as possible. We have created a valuable package of information, inspiration and influence, and it is our responsibility to make sure the people who can benefit from it are made aware of it.

'I still haven't done much at all in the way of marketing. Luckily, without my input the book is doing well. It has five-star reviews on Amazon and is also given to all new starters on a VA training programme as a part of their course. A year in, I broke even on costs (not time, obviously, but actual paid out money) and it's still getting reviews. What makes me glad I did it is the number of people who have got in touch to say how much it helped them or how much they enjoyed it. That is the best feeling in the world.'

Kathy Soulsby, author *Virtually Painless*

One of the benefits of our book is that it's much easier to promote as a separate entity to ourselves, allowing us to avoid that 'look at me, I'm so great' type of self-promotion that many men seem much more comfortable with than we women do. By talking about the content of the book, and allowing others to give their positive views, we can be authoritative and influential without feeling unduly boastful and self-aggrandising.

'I don't have a lot of confidence in selling myself. And the nature of my business is it is me I'm selling: I'm the coach and trainer and facilitator and it's stuff I've developed. But I can promote a book, or I can give away a book. Or say, "Oh look, I've written a book." And that is impressive to people, because it's not easy to write a book.'

Antoinette Oglethorpe, author *Grow Your Geeks*

Here are six ideas for promoting your book on a consistent basis over the year from publication – none of which involve putting yourself out there in an uncomfortably pushy sort of way:

1. Buy a minimum of 250 copies of your book (you should have an author discount price from a publisher or printer that makes this affordable), and mail out one copy every weekday for a year. Make a list that includes: prospects (your ideal potential clients); key people of influence in your market or industry who might otherwise be hard to make contact with (it's amazing how people respond to you as the author of a high-quality book); current and previous clients who can be encouraged to refer you, and your book, to their contacts; organisers of industry events in this country and overseas, who could offer you speaking gigs or to sit on expert panels; people in the media, from producers of high-profile TV programmes to local radio stations, newspapers and journals, offering appearances, articles, etc from an expert perspective; bloggers, YouTubers, podcasters, Facebook Livers who might want to interview you on their platforms.

You are likely to be amazed at how much interest and value you get from posting one book out each day. If you're offered interviews and speaking gigs, take them.

'I think one of the biggest challenges women face after
writing a book is to feel comfortable promoting it. I know I
felt very self-conscious and worried about how my network
would perceive me if I regularly promoted it, and myself
by association. Writing my book has helped me gain the
confidence and clarity I needed to share my expertise
with others. Some of my clients tell me that reading my
book was an important factor in deciding to work with me
because they felt like they knew me.'

2. Thirty days after your book has appeared on Kindle, run a 99p
price promotion on KDP Select and ask all your social media contacts, email list, friends, family, colleagues – every single person you
know – to download a copy and promote your offer until you reach
a #1 Best Seller ranking in at least one category on Amazon. Then
screenshot your book's #1 position and post it all over social media.
The sales are not going to make you much in the way of royalties, but
you'll have had a reason to tell everyone you know about your new
book, and if you make it into the top ten of one of your categories,
you can call yourself an Amazon #1 best selling author for ever after.

3. Host a launch event for your book (schedule it after the Amazon
Best Seller Launch) as a great opportunity to contact other key
people of influence and media in your market, prospects, clients
and potential partners. Bear in mind that even though a book
launch doesn't have to be a complex or expensive event, the better
planned it is, the more effective and enjoyable it will be.

Ask one or two people with some influence in the area of your book (it could be your publisher, a key person of influence in your business area, a more experienced author) to say something introductory, congratulatory and, above all, brief about you and your book. Your own speech should be the last one: in essence, it should be a pitch for your book (and your business or brand), your reasons for writing, who should read it and your aspirations for it – with loads of thanks thrown in (again, five minutes max). Have a photographer, professional or amateur, taking photos throughout the event (people love to see pictures of themselves on social media), but especially of the speeches. And make sure another supporter is videoing all the speeches. Upload the videos, especially yours about the book, to YouTube and link to it from your Author Page on Amazon, as well as your website and other social media. End your talk (leaving a pause after the applause, so this bit can be edited out of your video – or get someone else to say this) by saying you will now be signing books and they are on sale at a great discount this evening.

Make sure you've prepared a table and a system – with at least two helpers – where people can queue to buy copies of the book (the helpers need to be in charge of this and should have a float for giving change); then guests move along the table to get their purchased books signed by you. Make sure that you've ordered in a good supply of books in good time. This may take you through to the end of the event – after which you can relax and bask in the glow of your celebration. Don't forget to follow up any leads and introductions the next day; book launches are always a networking opportunity, including for the author.

You can watch a great example of a book launch video for Caroline Flanagan's *Baby Proof Your Career* here: https://youtube/flFi1Kq2eEc

4. Whether you already have a blog or need to start one, re-purpose the content of your book into blog posts, promote the blog posts on social media and link the posts back to your Amazon page so followers who want more can find the book to read.

> 'We all wonder whether the market can take another book on business or leadership or coaching. What we forget is that we all are unique and we all have our own unique way of presenting and communicating. We are doing the world a disservice if we don't get up there and say it our way.'

5. Start a podcast on the subject of your book, and interview other influencers and authors. Send them a copy of your book as an introduction. Alison Jones has built the Extraordinary Business Book Club podcast in conjunction with her book, *This Book Means Business.*

> 'The podcast originally started as a sort of heavy-handed accountability strategy and to get some primary material. It was a research tool for the book, but it's taken on a life of its own, and it has given me a new status and following, which has brought lots of high-end clients in. It's really interesting and it's huge fun to do. And I've learned a huge

amount myself, which is always good. But I wouldn't have started the podcast if I hadn't needed to kick myself up the backside to finish the book.'

Alison Jones, author *This Book Means Business*

Just as I believe we have a responsibility to write and publish our books, to establish our authority as experts in our field on an equal basis with the male authors and experts, so we need to step up and promote those great and powerful books. If the aim is in part to increase the authority base of women in business, we can't afford to be shrinking violets about the work we've created. If you need inspiration to step up and put yourself out there via your book, think of your readers, your clients, your colleagues and your daughters, who will all benefit from the world knowing more about your expertise and experience. And although 'marketing' sounds like a scary activity and 'selling ourselves' is not something we always feel comfortable with, appreciation, praise and a bit of the limelight can feed our spirits and build our confidence to go on to greater things.

6. Wait for about three months after your paperback and e-book have been published, and then record the audiobook to add the third increasingly important format. Unless you have a speaking voice that is really hard to understand, read your own book rather than pay a professional voice artist to do it. A good studio, producer and editor will support you through the process and make you sound professional and engaging.

Your readers/listeners want to get to know you, so an audiobook is another opportunity for you to have a direct conversation with your ideal clients and supporters. Make sure your manuscript is edited into an audio script, so you don't trip up over sentences that read well but sound unnatural, or end up saying things like, 'The following illustration shows you…'

Audible (ACX) is demanding about the quality of recordings and has specific ways it wants the files packaged. It's worth making sure you get this done professionally, as if Audible rejects your recordings, you may have to re-record, re-edit and/or re-package, which adds to the cost and time.

Increasingly the consumers of business books expect and enjoy an audio version; it doesn't appear to reduce sales of other formats – often a listener will then download the Kindle or paperback version for reference or to pass on. And the royalties on your audiobook are higher than for other formats.

If you still feel uncomfortable about promoting your book, Daniel Priestley makes this point:

> 'Any business book author, and perhaps this is especially reassuring for women who don't enjoy self-promotion, needs to understand that it's not their job to promote the book. The book promotes you and your business – it goes out working 24/7 and gets to people you won't ever have time or be in the right place to meet. You'll

make far more money from the books you give away
than those you sell.'

If you work through all these steps, planning, scheduling and
chunking down each task so it becomes discrete and manageable,
there is no reason why you can't get a really powerful business or
self-development book written and published. You will come out
of the process with an archive of content in your head as well as
on the page, and with an authoritative place in your industry.
Your friends, family and colleagues will be proud of you, and if
your Angel in the House returns with a gin hangover, she will
only be a little sour that you managed to achieve this impressive
task without her help. The ABOO Circle will welcome you with
open arms and ask you to encourage other women to write their
book. Be ready for your business to take off in obvious and sur-
prising ways, as members of the ABOO Circle have found:

> 'Writing my book has been the single most important thing
> I've done in my business.'

> 'Not least, your individual book will have added to the total
> sum of respect for women in a world where we are still
> fighting for acknowledgement.'

> 'Just do it – it's really the best business decision, the most
> empowering, challenging and rewarding thing you can ever
> do.'

Conclusion

'You've always had the power, my dear, you just had to learn it for yourself.'
Glinda the Good Witch, The Wizard of Oz

I very much hope that in a few years' time, *A Book of One's Own* will read like a dated relic of a bygone age because equal numbers of women as men will be starting their businesses, accessing funding to grow their companies, confidently writing their award-winning business books and leveraging them to increase their impact, influence and income.

In the meantime, being aware that many – not just a few – of us continue to struggle with undervaluation, conscious and un-conscious bias, and a perceived lack of authority in business and writing, may give us a sense of solidarity and the desire to encour-age each other to overcome these barriers. If you are the author of a business book, and would like to offer advice and support to women on the journey to a book of their own, please join us on the ABOO – A Book of One's Own secret Facebook group. Message me and give me your details so I can add you – we will welcome your input whether regular or occasional.

We may not have the individual power to change the current societal norms within which we operate, but we can be aware of the ABOO Archetypes who can help and hinder us in our book-writing process.

Professor E Tory Higgins' Regulatory Fit Theory tells us we make good decisions about achieving goals based on the right balance of two types of motivation: *promotion-focus* attracts us to the hopes, accomplishments and gains of a project; *prevention-focus* concentrates on security, safety, responsibilities and 'non-losses'.[40] It seems that as women we are more susceptible to prevention-focus when considering projects like writing our book – as represented by the Risk Assessor.

Our internal Risk Assessor has strong prevention-focus and is on constant alert for potential downsides to any action. When our book ticks too many boxes on her clipboard, we have to focus her attention on the risks of not writing and publishing our book – the loss of authority, opportunity and income, failure to grow our self-confidence and make a difference to our readers, market and gender.

---

40 http://psycnet.apa.org/doiLanding?doi=10.1037%2F0003-066X. 55.11.1217

The Impostor sometimes partners with the Risk Assessor to make us believe our book will be ignored or criticised, and we'll be judged for our views, opinions and even for thinking we could do this. It helps to remember that 70% of successful people suffer from Impostor Syndrome – and the other 30% just don't admit to it.

If you can't quell your Impostor on your own, turn to The Mentor for support, reassurance and promotion-focus. She could be someone in your ABOO Circle, an informal champion or a professional writing or book coach or mentor. We know that women feel the lack of professional support networks, especially if they work alone or run their own business, but respond very positively to other women mentors.

We also feel supported and encouraged when working in groups, so consider starting your own ABOO Circle.

While you're writing a book of your own, it's important to take a break from at least some of your perceived responsibilities as everyone's Big Sister, at work as well as at home. Although you may feel indispensable, it can be a good time to ask others – colleagues, partners, children – to step up and own some responsibility in a way that will benefit them as well as you.

If you're in Cinderella mode – struggling with cashflow and home responsibilities – take it easy, take support where you can and be real- istic about what you can achieve and when. If the book is too big a project to take on at the moment, start or maintain regular blogging or arti- cle-writing until you know you have enough content and time to pull it all together into your book. Talk up your book and authorship to give yourself confidence and authority when you're out at the networking ball.

Beyoncé's rendition of BC Jean's song 'If I Were A Boy'[41] says it all in the first few lines. How many of us can comfortably roll out of bed in the morning, throw on whatever clothes come to hand and go out into our (business) day with sublime confidence? Most of us are equally unable to put ourselves first and make up the rules as we go. But we don't have to be boys or men – it's our job, right here, right now, to ensure that we women are simply the successful equals of our male twins.

The Angel will try her best to recall you from that particular mission. Her vision of a woman's role is to be subservient, quiet, and to focus on the needs of others. She is the one who tries to make you anxious about being seen as pushy or self-serving, wary of getting above yourself or inappropriately self-confident. She speaks through others and directly to you when you're alone. Stand up to her – her time is over and yours is now.

---

41   https://en.wikipedia.org/wiki/If_I_Were_a_Boy

You can muster the combined forces of Miss Moneypenny and The Librarian. Working together they can enable you to create, compost and structure your book over time, plan your writing schedule around your work and home commitments, and use your experience of multi-tasking to minimise the short-term disruption while you make this important project happen.

With the information in *A Book of One's Own*, the support of a Mentor and the ABOO Circle, you can become a Hero sooner and more easily than you think. If you haven't started your book yet, step up and step into the arena where you can deploy your strength and your skill. Once it's written and published, your book will act as both your sword and shield in the ongoing campaign for the influence, impact and income you will bring to yourself, your brand, your business, your family and your gender.

If you are a woman who has written or is writing your book and would like to share your experience, please take 10 minutes to complete the ABOO Survey at *bit.ly/ABOOSurvey*.

The results are updated regularly on *lucymccarraher.com* and I may get in touch about recording an interview for the A Book of One's Own podcast.

If it's time for you to plan, write and publish a book of your own, contact me on Facebook, Twitter or LinkedIn to join the ABOO – A Book of One's Own Facebook group, find a Mentor and/or set up your own ABOO Circle.

abookofonesown.co.uk
Facebook.com/LucyMcCarraher
Twitter.com/lucymccarraher
linkedin.com/in/lucymccarraher

Further Reading

The Confidence Code: The science and art of self-assurance – what women should know, Claire Shipman and Katty Kay, HarperCollins 2018

The Eldest Daughter Effect: How First Born Women – like Oprah Winfrey, Sheryl Sandberg, JK Rowling and Beyoncé – Harness their Strengths, Lisette Schuitemaker and Weis Enthoven, Findhorn Press 2016

Executive Function: Cognitive Fitness for Business, Keiron Sparrowhawk, LID Publishing 2016

Feel The Fear And Do It Anyway: How to Turn Your Fear and Indecision into Confidence and Action, Susan Jeffers, 25th edition, Ebury Publishing 2012

The Female Eunuch, Germaine Greer, Relaunch Edition, Harper Perennial 2006

How To Own the Room: Women and the art of brilliant speaking, Viv Groskop, Bantam Press 2018

How To Write Your Book Without The Fuss, Lucy McCarraher and Joe Gregory, Rethink Press 2015

IN Security: Why a Failure to Attract and Retain Women in Cybersecurity is Making Us All Less Safe, Jane Frankland, Rethink Press 2017

Key Person Of Influence, Daniel Priestley, Rethink Press 2014

Lean In: Women, Work, and the Will to Lead, Sheryl Sandberg, W H Allen 2015

The Paula Principle: Why Women Lose Out at Work – And What Needs to Be Done about It, Tom Schuller, Scribe Us 2018

The Power, Naomi Alderman, Penguin 2017

A Room Of One's Own and Three Guineas, Virginia Woolf, 2nd Edition, OUP Oxford 2015

Thinking, Fast And Slow, Daniel Kahneman, Reprint Edition, Penguin 2012

Women & Power: A Manifesto, Mary Beard, Profile Books 2017

Women Don't Ask: Negotiation and the Gender Divide, Linda Babcock and Sara Laschever, Princeton University Press 2003

Work Like a Woman: A Manifesto For Change, Mary Portas, Bantam Press 2018

The ABOO Circle

Michele Attias, *Look Inside: Stop Seeking Start Living*

Lucy Barkas, *Leader X: How Generation X leaders are changing business for good*

Sue Belton *Change Your Life in Five – Take back control. Be brave. Enjoy the ride.*

Sherry Bevan, *The Confident Mother: A collection of learnings with excerpts of interviews from the 2015 The Confident Mother online conference*

Lyn Bromley, *Trusted: The human approach to building outstanding client relationships in a digitised world*

Audrey Chapman, *Love Selling – How To Sell Without Selling Out*

Antoinette Dale Henderson, *Leading with Gravitas: Unlock the six keys to impact and influence*

Jane Duncan Rogers, *Before I Go: The Essential Guide to Creating A Good End of Life Plan*

Nina Farr, *I am the Parent Who Stayed, Joyfully Parenting Alone*

Jane Frankland, *IN Security: Why a Failure to Attract and Retain Women in Cybersecurity is Making Us All Less Safe*

Cai Graham, *The Teen Toolbox: Equipping Parents and Teenagers with the Tools for Navigating Adolescence*

Karen Green, *Recipe for Success: The ingredients of a profitable food business*

Tara Halliday, *Unmasking: The Coach's Guide to Impostor Syndrome*

Elizabeth Harrin, *Customer-Centric Project Management, Shortcuts to Success: Project Management in the Real World, Project Manager, Collaboration Tools for Project Managers*

Suzanne Hazelton, *Great Days at Work: How Positive Psychology can Transform Your Working Life*

Emma Heptonstall, *How to be a Lady Who Leaves: The Ultimate Guide to Getting Divorce Ready*

Fadela Hilali, *Stuffed: how to feel so good about yourself you won't have room for cake*

Sally Holloway, *The Serious Guide to Joke Writing*; as Sally J Duffell, *Grow your own HRT*

Kath Howard, not yet published

Sue Ingram, *Fire Well – How To Fire Staff So They Thank You*

Alison Jones, *This Book Means Business: Clever ways to plan and write a book that works harder for your business*

Joanne Jong, *The Fashion Switch – the new rules of the fashion business*

Stacey Kehoe, *Get Online: 6 simple steps to launching a digital marketing strategy for the non-tech savvy*

Barbara Khattri, *Make It Personal*

Ruth Kudzi, *Is This It? A Smart Woman's Guide To Finding Work You Love*

Sarah-Anne Lucas, *It's Never About the Fitness: 11 Daily Rituals to create a love-affair with your body*

Jane Malyon, *Scone or Scon(e) – the essential guide to British Afternoon Tea*

Lucy Matthews, *A Marvellous Reputation: 10 Lessons from My Life as a PR Insider for Entrepreneurs Who Want To Be Talked About*

Antoinette Oglethorpe, *Grow Your Geeks: A Handbook for Developing Leaders in High-Tech Organisations*

Monica Or, *Star Quality Hospitality – The Key to a Successful Hospitality Business, Star Quality Experience – The Hotelier's Guide to Creating Memorable Guest Journeys, Star Quality Talent – Inspiring Hospitality Careers*

Marianne Page, *Process to Profit – systemise your business to build a high performing team and gain more time, more control and more profit, Simple Logical Repeatable: Systemise like McDonald's to scale, sell or franchise your growing business*

Eve Poole, *Leadersmithing, Capitalism's Toxic Assumptions, Buying God, Ethical Leadership, The Church on Capitalism*

Janet Poot, *A Different Kind of Leader: Accelerating Progress in a World of Disruption*

Penny Pullan, *A Short Guide to Facilitating Risk Management, Business Analysis and Leadership, Virtual Leadership*

Lisette Schuitemaker, *Alight, The Eldest Daughter Effect, The Childhood Conclusions Fix, Childless Living*

Jacqueline Shakespeare, *The Mother, The Professional and Me*

Karen Skidmore, *Shiny, Shiny: How to Stop Being a Social Media Magpie*

Shireen Smith, *Legally Branded, Intellectual Property Revolution – Successfully manage your IP assets, protect your brand and add value to your business in the digital economy*

Kathy Soulsby, *Virtually Painless: The unedited reality of moving from Personal Assistant to Virtual Assistant, PA to VA, employee to business owner*

Leanne Spencer, *Rise and Shine, Remove the Guesswork*

Adele Stickland, *Hello Gorgeous – how to look and feel fantastic every day!*

Heidi Strickland-Clark, *Why Weight? How to be happy every day whatever the scales say*

Nadjeschda Taranczewski, *Conscious You: Become The Hero of Your Own Story*

Gillian Wagner, *Barnardo, Children of the Empire, The Chocolate Conscience, Thomas Coram, Gent. 1668 – 1751, Miss Palmer's Diary, The Secret Journals of a Victorian Lady*

Amanda C. Watts, *Escape, The Pioneering Practice*

Sandra Webber, *Own It – regain control and live life on your terms*

Donna Whitbrook, *Trusted: The human approach to building outstanding client relationships in a digitised world*

Liz Whitaker, *The Power of Personal – How to Connect, Convince, and Create Exceptional Client Relationships*

Wendy Whittaker-Large, *101 Essential Tips for Running a Professional HMO*

Jutta Wohlrab, *Happy Birthing Days – a midwife's secret for a joyful, safe and happy birth*

Vicki Wusche, *Using Other People's Money: How to invest in property, fourth edition 2016; Make More Money from Property: From investor thinking to a business mindset, second edition 2017; Property for the Next Generation, 2018; The New Estate: Insights from the 22nd Century, 2015; The Wealthy Retirement Plan*

Joy Zarine, *The Five Star Formula: Create Incredible Guest Experiences That Lead To Five Star Reviews And An Award Winning Hospitality Business*

Acknowledgements

A huge thank you to all the authors who contributed to this book by completing the ABOO Survey and being interviewed about their writing and publishing experience. Your openness and honesty are much appreciated, and your insights and encouragement will help other ABOO authors enormously.

Thank you, as ever, to my business partners, Joe Gregory and Daniel Priestley, for their support throughout and valuable contributions in and outside the book. Much appreciation to Shaa Wasmund for writing the Foreword.

The Business Book Awards were the catalyst for the writing of *A Book of One's Own*, and I'm grateful in so many ways to the BBA team at Thinkfest, Safaraz Ali, Kasim Choudhry, Brad Edwards and Hannah Patel.

Virginia Woolf's *A Room of One's Own* was a starting point and an inspiration. I loved that her original cover design was created by her artist sister Vanessa Bell, and this inspired me to ask my feminist artist daughter-in-law Clementine Keith-Roach to create the cover for *A Book of One's Own*. I couldn't be happier with her stunning design.

The Rethink Press team have, as ever, been supportive, creative and efficient – it's reassuring to know that our process works as well for authors as I think it does from the other side. Verity Ridgman read as I wrote and helped me shape a much better book. Alison Jack contributed her usual insight and finesse in editing the manuscript. Jo Holloway proofread and gave support in so many ways. Kate Latham was not only a superb project manager but an enthusiastic early supporter. And Anke Ueberberg's oversight as our Operations Manager was as usual impeccable.

Last, but very much not least, love and gratitude to my husband Richard McCarraher and my mother Gillian Wagner; to my sons James Page and Christopher Page; my daughters Vika McCarraher and Julia McCarraher, and my other daughter-in-law Kate Lloyd. Charlie, Lucas and Rainer – this is a tiny contribution to a better world for you. Without all of you there would be nothing and no point. You probably don't realise how much you've helped me write *A Book of One's Own*.

The Author

Lucy McCarraher is the Co-founder and Managing Editor of Rethink Press. She is Publish Mentor for Dent Global and the international Key Person of Influence programme. In 2017, Lucy founded the Business Book Awards to celebrate the quality and variety of business books in the market.

She started her first publishing company while she was at university in Australia, and has been writing, editing and publishing ever since. She has been a magazine and book editor and publisher; print and TV journalist in Australia and the UK; a writers' agent, and an editor for Methuen. As Director of Development at Lifetime Productions International, she developed, wrote and script-edited UK and international TV and video series.

Lucy was a national expert in work-life balance, writing academic and business reports for clients and authoring *The Work-Life Manual* and *The Book of Balanced Living*. Her clients included multinational and blue-chip companies, including Virgin,

Microsoft and several banks, large public sector and voluntary organisations, and SMEs.

She is the author of twelve books, including *How To Write Your Book Without The Fuss*, with her business partner Joe Gregory, and *How To Write Fiction Without The Fuss*. Her first novel, *Blood and Water*, was published by Macmillan New Writing, followed by *Kindred Spirits* and *Mr Mikey's Ladies*. Lucy's self-help books include *A Simpler Life* and *The Real Secret*, both co-authored with social psychologist, Annabel Shaw.

She has a post-graduate diploma (DTLLS) in teaching Creative Writing and Literacy and speaks regularly about writing and publishing.

You can contact Lucy on:

www.lucymccarraher.com
Facebook.com/LucyMcCarraher
Twitter.com/lucymccarraher
linkedin.com/in/lucymccarraher